How Would God REALLY Vote?

A Jewish rebuttal to
David Klinghoffer's
conservative polemic

**Larry Yudelson
& Yori Yanover**

Ben Yehuda Press
Teaneck, New Jersey

Published by Ben Yehuda Press
430 Kensington Road
Teaneck, NJ 07666

http://www.BenYehudaPress.com

Ben Yehuda Press books may be purchased for educational, business or sales promotional use. For information, please contact:
Special Markets, Ben Yehuda Press,
430 Kensington Road, Teaneck, NJ 07666.

markets@BenYehudaPress.com.

pb ISBN   1-934730-19-X
pb ISBN13 978-1-934730-19-5

Library of Congress Control Number & CIP pending

08 09 10   / 10 9 8 7 6 5 4 3 2

For Yael Sarah,
      Ariella Rebeccah,
      Samuel Mitchell,
      Joseph Andrew
and Ruth Sophie
      — L.Y.

For Yarden and Nancy
      — Y.Y.

Contents

Acknowledgements

By the Grace of God,
and with a lot of help from my friends

First, and least adequately, love and gratitude to Eve, my partner, friend, editor and wife. Some women tolerate their husbands tilting at windmills; you come along for the ride. Much of this book, particularly in chapters four and five, reflect our conversations, now stretching over nearly a quarter of a century. All of it reflects your well-honed ear, your sharp editorial eye, and your deep commitment to Judaism, humanity, and literary excellence.

My parents and teachers, B.J. and Julian Yudelson, taught me to love Torah and to love America; I hope they understand that I have inherited their passions, even if we may disagree on interpretations.

Special thanks to Yori Yanover, for joining in this crazy endeavor with his usual full-throated enthusiasm, erudition and wit. If you like his work on this book, you'll *love* his new novel, THE CABALIST'S DAUGHTER. A special shout-out to friends whose insights, advice and email camaraderie helped this book come to fruition, and helped me maintain my sanity along the way: Alan Brill, Bob Carroll, and Andrew Silow-Carroll.

A name check to those bloggers who kept their vision clear and their prose steady when last-century institutions as august as *The New York Times* decided the agnosticism on the debate between biologists and creationists was the best way to increase circulation in 21st century Evangelical America and that "evenhandedness" was more important than a quest for the truth: TalkingPointsMemo, TheAgitator, Talk2Action, Orcinus, Pharyngula and Digby's Hullabaloo, to name the first that come to mind.

This book would not exist were it not for J.J. Goldberg, former editor of the weekly *Forward* newspaper, who hired David Klinghoffer to write a monthly column which added more heat than light to the Jewish communal debate. Acknowledgement must be made as well to David Klinghoffer, who has been nothing less than a gentleman in the few brief email exchanges we have had. Were he not so profoundly *wrong*, this book would not have been necessary.

Until third grade, I hated writing with a passion. Karen Halbfinger, my English teacher at Cleveland's Agnon School, taught me that writing could be a pleasure. I promised myself at the time that I would dedicate my first book to her; I hope this acknowledgement suffices.

Instead, I've dedicated this book to my children. I would have liked them to grow up in an America where books such as this one were neither urgent nor necessary, but that was not up to me. Instead, I hope they accept this volume as a token of my conviction that the fight for the ideals of America and Judaism is always noble.

Larry Yudelson
August 21, 2008 / Av 20, 5768
Teaneck, New Jersey

How Would
God
Really Vote?

1

Why We Had To Write This Book, God Help Us

W hat is it about David Klinghoffer's book, *How Would God Vote? Why The Bible Commands You To be a Conservative* that demands a refutation? Why couldn't we, two traditional Jewish men with families and jobs, leave well enough alone? Why did we feel so compelled to write this book, anyway?

These are good questions. After all, Klinghoffer is not exactly Rush Limbaugh or Bill Bennet. There are certainly more famous and even more annoying conservatives out there, not to speak of better selling authors (we're thinking Ann Coulter).

There are also many other right-wing Jewish authors—too many, really. So why pay Klinghoffer the compliment of dedicating a book-length rebuttal to his work?

For starters, while some of his embarrassed ideological allies and smug ideological foes may find it convenient to dismiss Klinghoffer, that is far from a universal response. Until just before the publication of *How Would God Vote?*, Klinghoffer was a monthly columnist for *The Forward*, arguably the most prestigious op-ed page of any American Jewish publication. Klinghoffer has also expounded on the intersection of public policy and religious teachings in other publications, such as the *New York Jewish Week* and *Hadassah Magazine*. Make what you will of the quality of Klinghoffer's thought (and we'll be making plenty in the course of this book), Klinghoffer has been a "public intellectual" in the Jewish community at a time when few even aspire to the title.

Klinghoffer owes his spot in *The Forward* to Affirmative Action, as the token Republican Orthodox Jew in a paper that is neither. To our chagrin, those two identities have merged in America in the past thirty years, as Orthodox Jews and Republicans have become increasingly conservative and reactionary.

It is against that dismaying background that we must view Klinghoffer's new book, as it is the first full-length work that claims to lay out a traditional Jewish theology of fealty to the Bible Belt morality. Politicians no longer need limit their Jewish platform to the security of the State of Israel. Klinghoffer invites traditional Jews to embrace conservative values like useless government, restrictions on contraception and the idea that smoking is good for you.

You have to admire Klinghoffer's ambition, trying to sell the conservative package as Torah from Sinai. The problem: It's not, and we find intolerable the notion that the descendants of labor unionist and freedom marchers are being urged into the Moral Majority with pseudo-biblical arguments that would have made our sages wince.

Perhaps Klinghoffer deserves our praise for collecting his Judeo-Conservative ideas into a book, making a public statement from what had heretofore been relegated to whispered debates in the pews during the weekly sermon, and to disturbing blogs (and even more disturbing anonymous e-mails). Klinghoffer gave us an opportunity to state for the record what the Torah *does* have to say about some political issues.

We don't answer every single one of Klinghoffer's talking points. If

Klinghoffer wants to be nice to illegal aliens, or to advocate gun control, who are *we* to argue? But please do not misunderstand our failure to answer each one of Klinghoffer's assertions to signify our assent— better the blanket belief that our silence on any one point is the result of time constraints. Deadline pressures forced us to limit the scope of our responses. A full rebuttal of all of Klinghoffer's errors of commission and omission could fill a much larger volume than this. Our project commenced following the publication of *How Would God Vote?*, in June, 2008, and since this book was to be published in time for the August Democratic convention, there was only so much ground we could cover.

In our rush to pursue justice, mistakes were surely made, but we stand firmly by our positions. Had we more time, we would have surely written a longer book.

And had we more time, we may have smoothed out certain chapters which not only reflect the views of two different authors, but which joust at Klinghoffer's swaggering conservative theology from a dizzying variety of directions. Sometimes we quarrel with his theology; other times we accuse him of the reckless use of strawmen. Sometimes we subject him to straightforward argument; other times we indulge in baroque flights of rabbinic fantasy. Would more consistency have made for smoother reading? Undoubtedly. Time constraints decided many editorial questions *for* us; we hope you'll let us get away with the occasional broad stroke.

We hope we have succeeded in conveying a sense that Torah—understood broadly to include rabbinic commentary—is not a conservative manifesto. Far from it. Where Klinghoffer (like Pat Robertson and company) sees the Bible as a call to wage a culture war in America, as a cudgel to pound everyone into his own image, we see the Torah as a tree of life, offering fragrant succor and a variety of enriching flavors, flowering like Aaron's staff.

Ultimately, it is our love of Torah *and* our love of controversy that led us to write this book. We were unwilling to stand by as our beloved Torah was maligned. Misrepresenting Torah, *ziyuf hatorah*, is a serious offense[1]. It is our hope that this book can serve as a *tikkun*, an antidote to the damage incurred by Klinghoffer's work.

Larry Yudelson and Yori Yanover

---

[1]   Schachter, Hershel, "Go Follow the Tracks of the Sheep," *Beit Yitzchak*, no. 17, New York, 1985, pp. 118-134..

2

Yes, But Is It Jewish?

The most disturbing aspect of David Klinghoffer's book, which claims legitimacy as the work of an avowed Orthodox Jew, is that it is simply not Jewish. Certainly it was not written in the spirit of our rabbinic tradition.

In his opening chapter, "With God or Against Him," Klinghoffer sets up a premise that's hard to follow, not because of its complexity, but because of what we on the Lower East Side would call a *mishmash* of concepts:

> It should go without saying that my political reading of the Bible is my own, drawing on the oldest biblical interpretive tradition, claiming roots that go back three thousand years and found in the Talmud and other ancient rabbinic texts. Yet Scripture's vision of

the ideal society does not belong to Jews alone.[1]

The paragraph reminded me of the old Jewish joke, which is better spoken, but since I don't know most of you personally, you'll have to do the voices in your head:

> A gentile professor of Judaic Studies in Iowa finds out that to really learn the Talmud he must go to the Boro Park section of Brooklyn and find himself a teacher. The professor flies over and knocks on a basement door and this little Jew comes out. Upon seeing him, the professor asks to be taught the Talmud, but the little Jews says, "I can't teach you Talmud, you got a *goyeshe kop*, you just don't think Jewish."
>
> The professor insists. The little Jew says, "OK, solve this problem, and I'll teach you:
>
> "Two people go down a chimney. One stays clean, the other gets completely *schmutzig*, filthy. Which one washes up?"
>
> The professor eagerly answers, "The dirty one, naturally."
>
> The little Jew wails: *"Goyeshe kop, goyeshe kop!* I *told* you I can't teach you anything. Listen, the *schmutzig* guy sees the clean guy. *Schmutzig* doesn't see any problem. But the clean guy sees the *schmutzig* guy and figures *he* must be just as dirty, so he goes and washes. I told you, you got a *goyeshe kop*. I can't help you."
>
> The professor begs for another chance, and the little Jew gives in, suggesting a new problem to solve:
>
> "Two people go down a chimney. One stays clean, the other gets completely *schmutzig*. Which one of them would wash up?"
>
> The professor says, "Sure, I know this one, it's the

---

[1] Klinghoffer, p.5.

clean fellow."

At this, the little Jew wails, *"Goyeshe kop,* the clean one takes a look at the dirty one and says, Moishe, you're all *schmutzig,* go wash already! Enough. I really can't help you, mister, you got a *goyeshe kop."*

The professor begs for one last chance, and the little Jews says, "Fine, one last chance, I'll give you a completely new problem, then you'll leave me alone:

"Two people go down a chimney. One stays clean, the other gets completely *schmutzig.* Which one of them washes up?"

At this point, if you're telling this joke, it's all physical stuff, as the poor professor from Iowa freezes, unable to decide which of the two conflicting solutions to choose. The little Jew can't stand it anymore and interjects, *"Goyeshe kop,* who ever heard of two people going down a chimney and only *one* of them gets *schmutzig?"*

For me, this joke illustrates the essence of Rabbinic Judaism. Hardly interested in developing uniform answers or dogmas, Rabbinic Jews love dispute, which enshrines all opinions. We actually celebrate the Talmud's pluralism with the declaration: *These and these, too, are the words of a living God* (Eruv. 13b, Gitin 6b, to name just two out of hundreds).

How can Klinghoffer say that he represents a tradition of 3000 years of rabbinic interpretation and in the same breath claim that there's such a specific thing as "Scripture's vision?"

When you read Klinghoffer's book—and the one now in your hands, too—keep in mind the image of the little Boro Park Jew, his hands raised to the heavens, wailing: *"Goyeshe kop!"* Because, to be honest, someone who has internalized the free spirit of our rabbinic sages would not seriously try to classify them either as right-wing conservatives, or as left-wing liberals.

The legal foundation for rabbinic law is found in Deuteronomy 17:8-10:

> If some issue is beyond your understanding, be-
> tween blood and blood, between plea and plea, and
> between stroke and stroke, as it might be a matter of
> controversy for you, then you will go up to the place
> which God chooses, and inquire with the priests the
> Levites, and with the judge that will rule in your days.
> And they will show you the sentence of judgment. And
> you will follow their sentence, given in the place which
> God will choose, and you will observe to do according
> to all that they instruct you.

In other words, if something comes up which is too difficult for you to decide on your own, go ask somebody who knows.

This dovetails nicely with the Mishna's recommendation: *Aseh l'cha rav*, "Appoint for *yourself* a master and a mentor." This phrasing indicates that you are an intrinsic part of the equation and that the arbiter you choose should be one who knows and understands you and your circumstances.

These two combined ideas, that you should seek advice on stuff you can't figure out for yourself, and that the advice you seek should come from someone who knows you, suggest that the average Joe in Torah Land is a highly intuitive person and well versed in the law, who follows his personal notions and personal path, except when he gets stuck.

We are encouraged to act independently and intuitively concerning the entire gamut of Torah law—in matters large and small. The phrasing of the text (Deuteronomy 17:8) is *ki yipaleh mimcha*, lit.: "Should it be too wondrous for *you*." This suggests a reliance for deciding proper behavior based on relative intuition, rather than strict knowledge.

This extremely individualized approach to morality and the law is profoundly emphasized when the Mishna describes wealth as a function of individual's assessment of his own satisfaction rather than some arbitrary number of gold pieces in his coffers. In the Mishna's view: *Eizaehu Ashir? Hasame'ach b'chelko.* "Who is wealthy? One who is content with his share." (Avot 4)

Indeed, I would define the rabbinic view on politics as the sanctification of Life, Liberty, and the Pursuit of Contentment. (Could this be characterized as a conservative idea?)

If the Torah envisions us as independent thinkers, each pursuing a personal definition of material well being, how could it possibly advocate a party line, whether conservative Republican or liberal Democratic? It stands to reason that, at its core, the Torah would encourage us to examine which of the two choices best matches our individual political needs and aspirations and vote accordingly.

In that sense, abortion is not a "yes" or "no" issue, to be decided on a strictly dogmatic basis, but an issue that reflects conflicting public needs. Likewise, every topic Klinghoffer deals with in his book, from women's issues to gay marriages to state-run schools to taxes to war, should be examined not according to dogma, but according to needs.

This pragmatic approach to politics rejects ideological litmus tests from the left, too. (This is why the American political system, with its direct voting for a local representative, is much more in line with rabbinic tradition than the Israeli system, in which one votes for a slate, often one based on ideology.) Government's job is to help improve my living conditions, *not* my morality.

In this context, let me note Klinghoffer's side comment in the first chapter praising the Bush Administration's seeking to "keep the brain-damaged Terri Schiavo from being dehydrated to death."

The very notion of discarding medical opinion and a spouse's decision based on competing ideology makes a mockery of our notion of free will. Of course, morality should be considered in decisions concerning euthanasia—but the idea that an individual's authentic, intuitive and cognitive struggle be hijacked by a moralizing government strikes me as alarmingly belligerent. If this is Klinghoffer's City on a Hill, I'll stay in the valley, thank you.

Klinghoffer's views on the relationship between Christians and Jews are just as disturbing. He writes:

> As an Orthodox Jew, I offer this book as a call to arms to America's mostly Christian conservative voters. [2]

And:

> John McCain was right when he said, in a 2000 interview on beliefnet.com, that our "nation was founded primarily on Christian principles.[3]" That fact should have practical consequences.[4]

Klinghoffer proceeds to contrast these views with those of whom he dubs the "New Atheists." But I suspect that inside the Orthodox Jewish world, Klinghoffer would have a hard time convincing anyone of the need to apply "practical consequences" to the Christian principles upon which this country was, supposedly, founded.

He would likely hear angry grumbling on topics like the Crusades, during which Christian zealots decimated Jewish communities. He might hear a thing or two about how the Inquisition applied its Christian values to destroy the thriving Jewish centers of Spain and Portugal. Or he might hear about the European Holocaust and our annihilation at the hands of our faithful Christian neighbors. Pope Pious XII's name might pop up in that context, as an example of how conservative Christian leaders responded when Jews were swept away in rivers of their own blood.

But even if we were to forgive Klinghoffer's imperfect awareness of

---

[2] Klinghoffer, p.2.
[3] McCain later clarified that he meant: "Judeo-Christian principles," which, if anything, is an even more problematic statement, for reasons which will follow.
[4] Klinghoffer, p.2.

Jewish history, the very assumption of such a thing as universally accepted Christian principles is patently wrong, just like the notion that the U.S. Constitution is based on them.

Klinghoffer must be familiar with historian Brooke Allen's popular book *Moral Minority* (Ivan R. Dee, 2007), in which she shows that the six most important founders—Franklin, Washington, Adams, Jefferson, Madison and Hamilton—were Enlightenment-style deists, who rejected the notion of making religion a basis for political life.[5]

They valued the separation of church and state. They devoted a passage in the US Constitution to eschewing religion as a basis for political life. They talked about God the "Divine Author" (Washington) or the "Superior Agent" (Jefferson). The Founding Fathers weren't atheists—*nobody* was in the 18th century. (Nobody except Thomas Paine, that is.) But to suggest that someone like George Washington would look to the Bible to "apply practical consequences" to political life is tantamount to telling a lie—which we have on reliable tradition that our first president was incapable of doing.

Putting aside the argument over historical revisionism, try Googling "Christian principles" and see if you can come up with any meaningful consensus. I couldn't.

Jewish principles are easier to pin down: Open a *siddur* (prayer book) and right after the morning service, you find Maimonides' Thirteen Principles of Faith. They are short, compact, and easy to remember —and there is even a rhyming version for sing-alongs.

Maybe Klinghoffer was spoiled by that gem of rabbinic marketing prowess and he figured the gentile prayer books offered a similar amenity. Fuggedaboutit. Everyone—from Marxist Catholics to Attila the Hun Evangelists—cites his own unique idea of Christian principles as the basis for his agenda. The Bible is a big book and there are enough verses to suit everyone's moral preferences. You want a couple of examples?

---

[5] See also *American Gospel: God, the Founding Fathers, and the Making of a Nation*, by Jon Meacham, Random House (2006) for similar arguments.

The National Council of Churches Justice and Advocacy Commission offers the following "Christian Principles in an Election Year:"

1. War is contrary to the will of God.

2. God calls us to live in communities shaped by peace and cooperation.

3. God created us for each other, and thus our security depends on the well being of our global neighbors.

4. God calls us to be advocates for those who are most vulnerable in our society.

5. Each human being is created in the image of God and is of infinite worth.

6. The earth belongs to God and is intrinsically good.

7. Christians have a biblical mandate to welcome strangers.

8. Those who follow Christ are called to heal the sick.

9. Because of the transforming power of God's grace, all humans are called to be in right relationship with each other.

On the other hand, a story on Ekklesia ("a think-tank that promotes transformative theological ideas in public life") from April 15, 2003, informs:

The Rev. Pat Robertson, the founder and chairman of the Christian Broadcasting Network and the Christian Coalition, said many Christians who support the war believe the biblical principles of loving one's enemy means that precautions must be taken to minimize civilian casualties.

"...As long as we continue the course we're on,"

Mr. Robertson said, referring to the overall concern
for Iraqi civilians, "we're on solid ground, not only in
terms of Christian, biblical concepts, but also in terms
of public relations."

As Iraqi casualties, by conservative counts, have reached a hundred
thousand (not to mention the countless injured and an estimated two
million displaced) one shudders at the projected magnitude of the
butchery had the good reverend *not* insisted upon minimizing civilian
suffering....

So, which are the *authentic* Christian principles that the U.S. is
founded upon? "Welcome the stranger," or "shoot every stranger that
moves?" Klinghoffer is not very specific here, although I suspect that
the kind of Christian principles he endorses would have driven Jesus
into one of his famous table-throwing tantrums.

But even if, somehow, the Bible Belt's Jesus Jumpers found common
Christian principles with St. John the Divine's watercress sandwich
crowd—which is one *big* IF—what resonance would these principles
have with religious Jews?

Having conjured the notion of universal Christian principles out
of whole cloth, Klinghoffer now moves on to another product of the
American imagination: "Judeo-Christian values."

...Pretending to fight "theocracy," secularists are
in fact attempting a radical redirection of American
life that seeks to silence the authentic Judeo-Christian
heritage that has sustained America since the country's
inception.[6]

Klinghoffer should read Arthur Allen Cohen's *The Myth of the Judeo-Christian Tradition* (Harper & Row, 1969), which questions the appro-
priateness of the term, theologically and historically, suggesting instead
that it is an invention of American politics.

[6] Klinghoffer, p.4.

Cohen thinks that there is simply no such thing as Judeo-Christian tradition. He points to the fact that the two religions have had separate theological agendas for the last two thousand years.

Or, if Klinghoffer prefers a gentile's opinion:

> The label "Judeo-Christian" tends to assume, at the expense of Judaism, that Christians and Jews believe essentially the same things. Besides glossing over the very real and important theological and liturgical differences, it tends to subsume Jewish traditions within an umbrella that is dominated by Christian ideas and practices.[7]

Let's be clear: Far from "sharing" one tradition, Orthodox Jews are prohibited from marrying Christians, setting foot inside a Christian church—and we can't even drink from an open bottle of *kosher* wine that has been used by a Christian. We reject the Christian idea of salvation, we abhor Christian divine teachings on every subject, and we are repulsed and outraged by incessant attempts by Christian missionaries to bring us into their fold.

It is particularly disturbing when Klinghoffer makes statements which reveal his complete assumption of elements of New Testament Pauline ideology, for instance, the requirement that wives submit to their husband's authority. There is no mandate on precisely how a woman should behave with her husband—Jews expect the happy couple to work it out for themselves. Also, while divorce may be a tragedy, and God cries, it is in no way banned—in Judaism, that is. The story in Christianity, and Klinghoffer's "Judeo-Christian Biblical America," is different.

Incidentally, we have more in common with Muslims than we do with Christians; Jewish law permits Jews to enter a mosque… but *not*

---

[7]   *Religion and the Workplace: Pluralism, Spirituality, Leadership,* by Douglas A. Hicks; Cambridge University Press, 2003)

a church.

To insist that we have some kind of bond with religious Christians because of similar core values, is to propagate a terrible lie. Christians who base their views on what they call the *Old Testament*, don't view Mosaic law as an abiding legal text. The Church has abolished Torah law as part of its attempt to abolish the very idea of Jewish nationhood.

> Pauline anti-Judaism seems not to be through the left hand as an implication of his Christology; rather his teaching on the law appears to be a spear in his right hand aimed straight at the heart of Judaism, that is, Torah… [Paul] does not disagree with individual Jews but with Judaism itself, saying that Christianity has replaced it. By attacking the law as such, Paul appears to attack not abuses and personal failings but the essence of Israel.[8]

Jews and Christians differ on every single fundamental principle—even on the meaning of core Scriptural texts. More crucially, Christians rely on the *Old Testament* for legal delineation; whereas Jews rely solely upon our rabbinic tradition. We never, *ever* turn to our Bible for legal guidance, *only* to our rabbinic literature. To suggest that our Sages had anything at all in common with the likes of Jerry Falwell, Jimmy Carter or Pat Robertson is a slap in the face of 2500 years of scholarship.

Judeo-Christian is as valid a concept as happy-joylessness, or tall dwarves. Klinghoffer's yearnings for this repugnant "ideal" is a deviant phenomenon without a trace of commonality in traditional Jewish thought, ancient or modern.

I have deep respect for religious leaders active in the interfaith arena, who seek to communicate and cooperate with Christians on political and social issues. But I resent Klinghoffer's attempt to erect an ideo-

---

[8]   *Paul and the Torah*, by Lloyd Gaston; University of British Columbia Press, 1987.

logical partnership between Christianity and its blameless victims.

David Klinghoffer attempts to rile up his readers through an attack on the "atheist left." In the process, he manages to break away from the very rabbinic Judaism he claims as his base. This book will attempt to correct his errors, which are numerous, not in an attempt to persuade readers that God's vote is with liberal lefties rather than with conservative righties, but, instead, to uphold our rabbinic tradition of multiple opinions. What this means in practice is that you can't cry "God says so" in a crowded town hall meeting.

3

His Is Not My Infinite God

Conservatives like David Klinghoffer pride themselves on being "tough-minded," pitting themselves against what they deride as "soft-headed, fuzzy-thinking" liberals. We accept that as an invitation to submit David Klinghoffer's *How Would God Vote?* to close scrutiny, and see how well its reasoning holds up.

Let's start with the first paragraph of the first chapter of his book:

> To anyone who takes God seriously, every election poses a radical question. Will we vote with Him, or against Him? The Bible is an unapologetically political book and an extremely conservative one. Some political views offend God, and those views are mostly liberal. To misperceive Scripture's political meaning is as

much an error as to misperceive its moral meaning. [1]

It has been said that Jews inevitably answer every question with a question. It is a habit we picked up from the Talmud. So let me ask: Does every election really hold that radical question? Is God actually on every ballot? One of my neighborhood Orthodox rabbis gave broad hints that citizens of my leafy New Jersey suburb[2] should vote for the town council slate proposed by the Orthodox mayor. Would it have been "against God" to vote for a different slate?

What about the local Democratic primary a month later? The ballot offered a choice between two competing slates for the county Democratic party. Was one slate with God, and one against? And what does that say about folks who chose to forgo the balloting altogether?

Do elections pose starker questions about God's choices than do any of our other activities? Can it be asked whether we are shopping with God, or against Him? Praying with God, or against Him? Driving with God, or against Him? Writing our books with God, or against Him? Is this question a radical one or—if taken seriously—merely part of the daily current of religious life?

More importantly, is Klinghoffer right in saying that there are always two clear alternatives?

He seems to make no sense—unless we charitably understand him to mean something different, which does make sense. What he appears to be asking is this: "To anyone who takes God seriously, every election [that offers a choice between a liberal candidate and a conservative candidate] poses a radical question. Will we vote with Him [for the conservative], or against Him [and for the liberal]?"

Thus amended, Klinghoffer's opening sentence makes sense. It is indeed a radical question. It is consistent with the entire thrust of Klinghoffer's book, whose methodology can be described simply thus: Con-

---

[1]   Klinghoffer, p.1.

[2]   For more on my leafy New Jersey suburb, see Rosenwein, Rifka, *Life in the Present Tense: Reflections on Family and Faith*, Teaneck: Ben Yehuda Press, 2007.

struct two straw men. Dress up one as a demonic, atheist liberal . Dress up the other as an angelic, Godly Conservative. Find a Biblical passage that supports the conservative straw man. Feel free to ignore contradictory Biblical passages. Conclude with a smile.

Truly, Klinghoffer burns through more straw men than a fireside production of *The Wizard of Oz*. As we proceed down the yellow brick road of *How Would God Vote?*, we'll wave at a few.

For now, let's note that Klinghoffer's primary thesis—that in every election it is a sin to vote for the liberal—is so absurd that he studiously avoided spelling it out directly.

Moving on, we reach Klinghoffer's third sentence ("The Bible is an unapologetically political book and an extremely conservative one.") We have to ask: Is the Bible *truly* a political book? For one thing, it is many books—twenty-four by my Jewish count, more for those who include the New Testament. And while the Jewish canon contains politics—which can be broadly defined as "social relations involving authority or power"—it contains far more than that, including poetry, history, and some rather stoic philosophy.

Shouldn't one at least consider the philosophy of Ecclesiastes?

> Vanity of vanities, all is vanity. What gains a man from all his labor at which he labors under the sun? One generation passes away, and another generation comes; but the earth abides for ever. [Ecclesiastes (aka Kohelet) 1:2-4]

Far from being a cry to vote either conservative or liberal, the Bible here seems to be making a strong case for staying home on election day, advising us to take the fleeting political circus a great deal less seriously. (Putting the electoral process into its proper perspective is probably healthy advice for the authors of this book and its readers, too—the actual voting entails a pleasant walk and can be a good break.)

Indeed, one can make the claim that the Bible is an unabashedly *apolitical* book—and that statement would be as true as Klinghoffer's.

Is the Bible an extremely conservative book?

Only if by conservative you mean preferring anarchy to monarchy, practicing radical land reform every 50 years[3], and coming out against the tax deduction for vacation homes.[4]

Do some political views offend God? In terms of clear Biblical verses, there are indeed some political views that God opposes. Most specifically, I'm thinking of some views very current in ancient Judea circa 586 b.c.e.[5] The kings of Judah allied themselves with Egypt to fight Babylonia, present-day Iraq. God was against the war: His prophets advocated seeking a humble, perhaps humiliating, peace. But while Jeremiah and some of his prophetic colleagues were wont to give explicit political advice to the Kings of Judah (who were wont not to take it), elsewhere the Bible in general, and the Torah in particular, tend to speak about individual religious practice, not political philosophy.

As we ponder the 2008 elections, God is playing things closer to the vest than He did 2600 years ago. With all due respect to David Klinghoffer, no bona fide prophet has come forth to channel God's voice on the issues of the day. (Jewish tradition reserves contemporary prophecy for "children and madmen."[6])

In the absence of a direct line to God, the question of which political views might offend Him is one that requires thought, study, and the interpretation of scripture and tradition. Like Klinghoffer, I have reached conclusions—informed by my study of Torah—about political matters. But, given the title of this book, it shouldn't surprise you that I reach conclusions that are diametrically opposed to his.

That we two Jews have reached conflicting opinions isn't really a big deal. I don't agree with Klinghoffer when he writes (last sentence of that first paragraph):

---

[3]   Leviticus 25:10-18

[4]   Amos 3:15 – see chapter 9 for a fuller discussion

[5]   That's how we Jews like to say b.c.—meaning Before Common Era, rather than the Christian term meaning Before Christ.

[6]   Talmud Baba Batra 12b

> To misperceive Scripture's political meaning is as
> much an error as to misperceive its moral meaning.

As a traditional Jew, I understand the challenge posed by Torah is one of action, not interpretation. I have been trained to ask: What am I commanded by Torah? In the main, I do not have to divine this on my own. The tradition (specifically the Talmud and its commentaries) distils 613 commandments from the Scripture that guide our daily practice. The Talmud is also clear about the ways in which the prophets, Isaiah, Micah and Amos, discovered the pithy essence of the Torah[7].

Klinghoffer's concern about the "error" of misperceiving scripture's "meaning"—political or moral—makes no sense from a Jewish perspective, because we understand the Torah to encompass multiple meanings. Arguments over just what the Torah means fill the 63 volumes of the Talmud, and the thousands of works of subsequent discussion.

As Americans, it may be wise for us to pause at this point to ask: If the Bible's meaning is not "self-evident" on all points, how can one justify imposing one individual interpretation upon the rest of the country?

This question, which cuts to the core of the intersection of religion and politics, of theology and political science, is flamboyantly ignored by Klinghoffer. To understand the import of this and similar questions, and their non-obvious answers, I recommend Mark Lilla's book, *The Stillborn God*, which Klinghoffer dismisses without opening. Lilla shows that there are no easy answers to these questions, but illustrates that some answers are bloodier than others. The doctrine of the separation of Church and State, which Klinghoffer blithely ignores, was deduced through the augury of much blood.

In particular, as Lilla indicates, America's Founding Fathers drafted an explicitly secular Constitution in response to the religious wars of Europe and England, in which the fights over Biblical interpretations were conducted on bloody battlefields.

---

[7]   Talmud Makkot 24a. See Chapter 15, "God's Platform," for details.

What Lilla calls "The Great Separation," that between Church and State, was only one historical response to the wars of Christendom. Another was the development of liberal religion, which argued that the difference between the correct interpretation and an incorrect interpretation was not the difference between Heaven and Hell. Such an approach has a graceful logic to it: If God wanted us to understand Him, wouldn't He have spoken so unequivocally that all could agree? This liberal approach also has the backing of the wisdom of the Talmud, which declared of the rival schools of Torah scholars, "Both these *and* these are the words of the Living God.[8]"

The practical solution to the problem of ascertaining God's will through Scripture lies in creating what theologians call "an interpretive community." That simply means that, generally speaking (and hypothetical Martian anthropologists aside) no reader is an island. People read Scripture as part of a community, and that community has a tradition of how to understand the Bible. The Catholic Church provided one such community for a thousand years, stamping out—sometimes brutally—members who interpreted God's will in ways unapproved by the Church. Rabbinic Judaism offered an alternative community.

The advantage of trying to understand the Bible in such a group is that by sharing common assumptions, a group can take some answers for granted even while disagreeing with each other on finer points. The interpretive community shares standards of logic, of language, of authority, of holiness, of accepted modes of revelation. To put it simply, Jewish and Christian theologians do not agree on what constitutes Sacred Writings. Our canon, the Tanakh, is called the Old Testament by Christians, who insist that Tanakh can only be understood through the New Testament. Jews counter by interpreting the Tanakh through the lens of the Talmud and Midrash. And so on.

This is where Klinghoffer commits his original sin. He poses as if he can speak as the definitive voice for the Bible for all Jews and all

---

[8]   Yes, I've translated the Hebrew ("*zeh v'zeh divrei elohim chayim*") differently than did my co-author in the previous chapter. That's exactly the point.

Christians. In doing so, he is really aligning himself with the community of Evangelical Protestants, a community which claims the right to read the Bible without a community.

Our claim as the authors of this present volume is more limited. We offer one Jewish reading of predominately Jewish texts. Make that two readings—we authors do not speak with one voice.

I understand Jewish texts—in particular, the Talmud and the Midrash—the classic Rabbinic writings of the 2nd-8th centuries—as making a strong argument against any singular interpretation of God's will. The Talmud is a virtual catalog of contradictory rabbis, arguments between Rav and Abaye as to what is the Jewish law in a given situation. In the Midrash we find multiple interpretations of Biblical passages, an array of possible ways to understand God's writing, God's will and God's plan. Later generations of rabbis discussed different topics—details of previously established laws and questions of philosophy, theosophy, and Biblical interpretation. Again, the rabbis energetically disagreed.

In the 19th century, the Hassisdic master Rabbi Zadok of Lublin drew a connection between the lack of unanimity in classical rabbinic literature, and the infinite nature of God. Yes, God is infinite; He is also, Judaism insists, One. God's unity is all-encompassing; it includes both the "nays" of the School of Shammai (generally stricter) and the "ayes" of the House of Hillel (generally more lenient). Only by embracing all views—each position and its opposite—can one begin to apprehend God. The God of Rabbi Zadok is a God of "both/and," not a God of "either/or."

This theology has a practical echo when considering the pluralistic nature of the United States of America. If the rabbis of the Talmud could not reach agreement on when to recite the morning prayer—and perhaps more importantly, *did not feel it necessary to reach agreement*—how should we expect 300 million Americans to reach agreement on what God demands from us, or even whether there is a God to place demands at all?

We approach the project of this book, then, with more humility than does Klinghoffer. We know there are many other interpretations of the Bible than those we present. And we are well aware that there are very strong arguments to be made against bringing the Bible into politics at all.

However, we could not leave Klinghoffer's blasphemous claim—that the Bible commands you to be conservative—unanswered.

One more point of disagreement as we get underway. Klinghoffer writes:

> John McCain was right when he said, in a 2000 in-terview on beliefnet.com, that our "nation was founded primarily on Christian principles."[9]

Our goal in this book is to argue theology, *not* political science. So I won't discuss the way in which this statement misconstrues the nature of America's founding, and of the founders' alleged Christianity.

But as a Jew, I want to make a point, one that may well be hard for conservative Christians to hear.

When I hear "Christian principles," I remember all the Jews who were tortured and killed—not to mentioned exiled—in the name of Christians' principles during the centuries in which Christianity was regnant in the West. I remember too the indigenous peoples who were victims of genocide in the Americas. And I remember how in the American South, "Christian" principles went hand-in-hand first with slavery and then with Apartheid.

Too often, the "Christian principle" was that the Christians were principal—and everyone else was secondary.

And when I hear talk of "Christian principles" coming from people directly connected to that form of Christian ethnic supremacy I am doubly suspicious. When *The National Review* advocated *for* segregation and *against* Martin Luther King, were *they* writing with God? Or against Him? And when the Republican party came to power ener-gized by a "Southern strategy" fueled by angered integration and the

---

[9] Klinghoffer, p.2.

forced end of American apartheid, was the Republican party with God, or against Him?

Really, to say that one candidate is radically *with* God and another radically *against* just doesn't seem true for most presidential elections. Unless, of course, you start factoring in questions of racism, of slavery, of the fundamental of human dignity and of respecting the Divine spark in everyone.

God is very "on message" about loving one's neighbor as oneself.

4

A Doom of Her Own: Is Anti-Feminism Jewish?

"The commonest worry about a biblically correct democracy is how women would fare," writes Klinghoffer.

Indeed.

Klinghoffer himself brings up matters of women's equality at the very beginning of his book. The ways that women's legal, social and economic rights have changed over the past century are front and center when Klinghoffer discusses how Biblical guidance would change America.

How honest is Klinghoffer when he reassures us that his proposed conservative Biblical utopia has nothing in common with, for instance, the Taliban's Islamic dystopia?

To understand Klinghoffer's policy prescriptions, you have to read him carefully. Don't take him at his word that what he wants would be "a far-cry from Taliban-style oppression." Note rather that he writes, "the place of women in an authentically scriptural government would be all about protecting freedom in the long term," and then listen carefully to how he defines freedom.

Because as Klinghoffer makes clear by the end of his chapter, he doesn't believe freedom for women means access to contraception, abortion or divorce—rights that modern American women take for granted.

"The Bible wants us to appreciate that women have more power in the traditional role than they will have, in the long run, if the traditional family is undercut by a legal system uninformed by scriptural wisdom," he says.

"Access to abortion and contraceptives similarly disempowers women," he says.

That's right. It's not really about abortion. It's about contraception.

Please do not assume that this ideology is limited to David Klinghoffer. President George W. Bush and Presidential Candidate John McCain also are part of the fight against birth control.

Six months before leaving office, the Bush administration proposed a regulation that, if implemented, would define many forms of birth control as abortion. As *The New York Times* reported:

> The Bush administration wants to require all recipients of aid under federal health programs to certify that they will not refuse to hire nurses and other providers who object to abortion and even certain types of birth control...
>
> In the proposal, obtained by *The New York Times*, the administration says it could cut off federal aid to individuals or entities that discriminate [sic] against people who object to abortion on the basis of "religious beliefs or moral convictions." The proposal defines abortion as follows: "any of the various procedures—including the prescription, dispensing and administration of any drug or

the performance of any procedure or any other action—that results in the termination of the life of a
human being in utero between conception and natural birth, whether before or after implantation."
Mary Jane Gallagher, president of the National Family
Planning and Reproductive Health Association, which
represents providers, said, "The proposed definition of
abortion is so broad that it would cover many types of
birth control, including oral contraceptives and emer-
gency contraception." [July 15, 2008]

Similarly, in 2007 then-Republican presidential candidate Mike
Huckabee said he wanted the federal government to ban the contra-
ceptive pill and other forms of birth control.

And in July 2008, Senator John McCain came under scrutiny for
voting several times in his career against expanding access to contraception—and then refusing to explain his position.

In short, contraception is indeed something that Klinghoffer and his
friends hope will go away—at least, in their vision of an America run
by their interpretation of the Bible.

It is worth considering why on earth contraception is becoming a
political issue. And it's worth asking: how would God *really* vote?

Now, part of the objection to contraception comes because Christians believe it recapitulates the sin of Onan. That's pretty much the
Catholic position. Unfortunately for Klinghoffer, Onanism does not
apply to women. Judaism *does* grant freedom of contraception to wom-
en. According to Jewish law, reproductive strictures apply to *men*, who
are bound by Jewish law to have children (at least two) and to not waste
their seed.

A second leg of conservative opposition to contraception is the belief
that the soul is introduced as soon as a sperm meets its egg. Theologically, that's a touchy situation, since 40% of fertilized eggs don't
reach the point of implantation. That's a lot of abortions God must be
performing! But from a Jewish viewpoint, as even David Klinghoffer

understands (and explains in his chapter on abortion), Judaism considers a fetus to have the status of a bodily fluid until several weeks after conception.

Pining for Patriarchy

So without a Jewish basis for joining Bush and McCain in opposing contraception, what is Klinghoffer's rationale? What is the third leg on which this position rests?

You won't hear it from the candidates, because McCain is out to win votes from ordinary Americans. But Klinghoffer is preaching to the Evangelicals. And if what he says is what they think, then Margaret Atwood's novel *The Handmaid's Tale*, with its oppressive Orwellian Christian government, is a pretty accurate reflection of what this core religious constituency really wants.

What it boils down to is this: Klinghoffer is an unapologetic supporter of patriarchy. He states forthrightly that, as he understands the Bible, the most important political unit is the *"Bet Av,"* "the parental house." That is a mistranslation, and doubly so, because it misstates the literal meaning of the phrase (deliberately, I believe) as well as its primary political meaning.

Literally, *Bet Av* means "father's house."

In that context, for example, Jacob prays to God to be able to return to his father's house (Genesis 28:21).

Or take Deuteronomy 22:20-21, referring to a bride whose groom accuses her of not being a virgin:

> If this thing is true, and the signs of virginity are not found for the girl; Then they shall bring out the girl to the door of her father's house, and the men of her city shall stone her with stones that she die; because she has perpetrated wantonness in Israel, to play the harlot in her father's house; so shall you put evil away from among you.

When Klinghoffer praises "the classical scriptural model of governance," is *this* the ideal of the parental house he wants to impose on America? And if not, what would he say are "the philosophic principles that animate that law", which he does not want to apply "dogmatically or simplemindedly"?

If America were ever to begin to cede its secular democracy to people like Klinghoffer—God forbid!—one man's dogmatism would become the next man's rule of law.

But while *Bet Av* literally means "father's house"—a grouping which, we see in references to the *Bet Av* of Abraham and Jacob, means the father, one or more wives, various children, and household slaves— Klinghoffer is simply wrong when he seizes on the term as evidence that the Bible values the familial unit.

In the political sense, and the only time the actual words *"Bet Av"* appear (as opposed to various possessive or plural cases) they refer not to the analogue of a nuclear family, but rather to a subdivision of a tribe. Perhaps clan would be a fair translation. In fact, the political unit of *Bet Av* is probably most alive today in tribal Afghanistan. There clans and tribes are the major political structure, and (not incidentally), the Taliban impose a theocracy and insist that women wear a Burka.

Needless to say, Talmudic and later rabbis, living in a society as far removed from Biblical tribal culture as is our own, recreate nothing resembling the *Bet Av* notion. Klinghoffer makes it up out of whole cloth.

And yet, perhaps *Bet Av* can be salvaged as a reference to family values. If I could be excused a Klinghoffer-style flight of fanciful Biblical interpretation, I might suggest that it is not insignificant that the only two individuals outside of the Levitical priesthood who are identified with a *Bet Av* are Zimri, the Simeonite prince and Cozbi, the Midanite princess who are caught *in flagrante delicto* and speared into *corpsus interruptus* by Pinchas the priest in Numbers 25 (as well as Klinghoffer chapter 15).

Using Klinghoffer's interpretation, is Scripture hinting that those who most loudly proclaim adherence to traditional "family values" may perhaps be the ones least likely to practice them? Following Kling-hoffer's lead we could translate Numbers 25:14-15 like this:

> And the name of the Israelite man who was struck, who was struck with the Midianitess, was Zimri, son of Salu, the prince of family values for the Simeonites. And the name of the Midianite woman who was struck was Kozbi daughter of Tzur, she was the head of mothers for family values in Midian.

Zimri then prefigures Congressmen Mark Foley, David Vitter, Larry Craig and Vito Fossella, who portrayed themselves as advocates of conservative family values—*nisiei bet av*, as it were—before being disgraced for harassing male pages, hiring a prostitute, soliciting in a men's room and fathering a child out of wedlock, respectively.

Women's Place, a la Klinghoffer

In Klinghoffer's conservative utopia women are "empowered" when they are kept at home, as mothers, and in marriages without divorce. Let's unpack the philosophical problems behind this approach to women.

In a word, it comes down to "essentialism," which is a fancy way of saying that Klinghoffer sees the essence of women being their women-ness. In his scheme, women's power exists in the family; outside the family, they have little or no existence.

It's easy to see how he could derive such a view from the Bible.

As in the verse from Deuteronomy we cited above, the accepted place of women in the Torah is as daughters, waiting to be married off (or sold as handmaidens) by their fathers, or as wives. In the institution of *Bet Av*, as Klinghoffer understands it, a woman must always be part of a man's *Bet Av*—a man's house.

This scheme precludes a woman being independent.

It is well known that conservatives, such as Karl Rove, idealize the administration of William McKinley. What may not be well known, but is apparent from reading Klinghoffer, is that one thing they admire about the 19th century is that it preceded women's suffrage. As true conservatives, they believe the arguments against giving women the vote.

And the key pillar of this is that a woman without a man is a nonesuch.

It can be hard to understand this, because of how thoroughly most of America has accepted the feminist arguments of the 1920s and the 1970s.

We take it for granted that a woman can vote, or can enter medical school.

We also take it for granted that women are referred to by their own names. We no longer read of a Mrs. Robert Kaputnik leading a women's group, though 40 years ago that was the standard style.

Conservatives argue that the changes of the 20th century which seem to be progressive were "really" steps backwards for women. (Fifty years ago conservatives made similar arguments against the Civil Rights movement which ended racial apartheid in America).

The liberal view is the most compelling: Women must first be treated as people. They are individuals, made in the Image of God. They are women second.

In Genesis 1, in the first, ribless story of creation, it says "male and female He created them." This denotes equivalence and equality between the male and female of the human species.

With this in mind, does it seem that Klinghoffer is right in his implicit claim that all women are truly empowered by being part of a male-led household?

Should the government really be telling girls that their happiness lies only with a man? Are women who have found happiness on their own simply deluded? Are they victims of "false consciousness," as the Communists used to say about people whose personal feelings didn't accord with official ideology?

Might it be that the Bible's portrayal of women mired in the household is a reflection of a moment in history and *not* an enduring philosophical principle?

Looking back at the passage about the non-virgin daughter in Deuteronomy, it is amazing that Klinghoffer decides such sentiments are eternal. After all, he says that not every commandment applies today. Why specifically hold on to antiquated views about women?

In rejecting "father's house" as a guiding principle of American life, and supporting the idea that we shouldn't push women back into the 19th century, I'm not just reading the Bible in a way that reflects my concerns for the well-being of my three daughters—I'm following the lead of the ancient rabbis.

It seems clear from the Biblical verse that fathers can marry off their daughters.

Not so, according to the Talmud.

The Talmud limited this parental prerogative to a particular six-month period. Younger, she was too young to be married. Older, she was a *bogeret*, an independent woman, responsible for her own marriage.

In other words, while *Bet Av* might have been a feature of Biblical life, it wasn't a feature of the world of the Talmud. In confining his reading of Judaism to the Bible and not continuing on with the Talmud, Klinghoffer joins in one of the cardinal theological sins of classical Christianity, namely: that of ignoring all of post-Biblical Judaism.

Klinghoffer looks to the story Adam and Eve as a guide to how all men and women should live their lives.

> Man and woman have opposite, separate roles–he going out into the world to work, compensating for the loss of Eden, she remaining in the home, reproducing Eden behind the doors of the family home. As Rabbi [Samson Raphael] Hirsch... notes in his commentary on the verses, this "certainly expresses no idea of sub-

ordination, but rather complete equality."[1]

Rabbi Hirsch, the 19th century Orthodox thinker, gets this much credit: He died 66 years before the U.S. Supreme Court affirmed "separate but equal" as an egalitarian fig-leaf to cover racial segregation. One would like to think that when Brown vs. Board of Education overturned that doctrine, he would not have joined Klinghoffer's publication—*The National Review*—in lamenting the decline of tradition wrought by making equality real.

Hirsch's views on women's place echoed those of his bourgeois German society. But they would have come as quite a shock to his younger (and more strictly Orthodox) contemporary, Rabbi Israel Meir Hacohen, who famously studied Torah while his wife ran a small grocery.

Sufferin' Suffragettes

What most 19th century, and most early 20th century, Orthodox rabbis would have agreed upon, however, is that women have no business voting or serving political office. Klinghoffer acknowledges that Maimonides would not let a woman run for president... but he backpedals: "the purpose of this book is to extract the philosophic principles that animate that [Biblical] law, not to apply them dogmatically or simplemindedly."

Huh?

Why doesn't Klinghoffer have the courage of his convictions to claim that Hillary Clinton defied God's will when she ran for president?

And why should we take Klinghoffer's arbitrary societal prescriptions more seriously than, well, Orthodox Jews today take last century's opposition to women's suffrage? Israel's Orthodox communities have all accepted woman's suffrage, insofar as they accept the idea of voting at all. And while a woman's role in ultra-Orthodox society is very different than those Hirsch defended and Klinghoffer would impose, suffrage seems not to have torn that society asunder.

As always, we're left asking the questions: How does Klinghoffer

[1] Klinghoffer, p.30.

draw his arbitrary line, and why should we trust him to run America?

Klinghoffer's idea, that there is one certain truth that can be teased from the Torah (a way of life that—miraculously!—coincides with conservative nostalgia for pre-Warren Court and pre-Roosevelt America) stands in stark contrast to the Talmudic view.

For the Talmud, there are always two sides to every issue.... and there is next to no coercive authority (i.e. governmental laws) on either side.

Indeed, the very story of Adam and Eve, as discussed by the Talmud (Berachot 61a), provides an example of how the ancient rabbis–our Sages of Blessed Memory–saw the Bible as a tool to elicit discussion, not impose conformity.

> R. Nahman b. R. Hisda expounded: What is meant by the text, "Then the Lord God formed (*"vayitzer"*)" man? The word *"vayitzer"* is written in the Torah with letters *yod*, to show that God created two inclinations, one good and the other evil....
>
> [No, the point of the two *yods*] is as explained by R. Jeremiah b. Eleazar; for R. Jeremiah b. Eleazar said: God created two countenances in the first man, as it says, Behind and before hast Thou formed me.

Let's look at this passage. Sparking this discussion is an apparent spelling mistake in the Torah: The word *"vayitzar"*, meaning "formed," is spelled with an extra letter. Since nothing in the Torah is accidental, this extra letter *yod* must teach us something. But what?

Rabbi Nahman offers an explanation, which is based on a Hebrew-language pun playing of *vayitzar* and *yetzer*, which means inclination. The doubled letter hints at the doubled nature of man: He has an inclination for good and an inclination for evil.

The "evil inclination" is generally understood to be sexual desire, and the Talmud isn't so sure that that is a bad thing. Where would the world be without sexual desire? So it suggests another explanation for the extra letter in "formed," along the lines of Rabbi Jeremiah. Rabbi Jeremiah also believes man to have been created double, but literally double, having two faces. This is the myth, more famous in Western culture from Plato, that the original man was a hermaphrodite, containing both male and females halves.

In reading the Talmud, it's easy to get confused by the flow of names and opinions. So let's pull back, and look at the two different views of the two rabbis. Both attribute to man a dual nature. In the first case, the dual nature is a moral duality: good and evil. In the second, the nature is sexual: male and female. Of course, both opinions are true. Man is good and evil, male and female. But note that the Talmud implicitly rejects the idea that the sexual duality corresponds to a moral duality.

Nothing so far explicitly contradicts Klinghoffer. But please note an important contrast. Klinghoffer, with his quote of Hirsch, implies that the Bible's meaning is clear. The Talmud, however, shows that the very first word in the story of the creation of Eve doesn't have a clear meaning.

The Talmud then recalls a similar debate over a slightly later verse:

> "And from the *tzela* [normally translated rib] which the Lord God had taken from man, he made a woman." (Gen. 2:22). Rav and Samuel explained this differently. One said that [this 'rib'] was a face, the other that it was a tail.

Here the debate is not over how to interpret a particular word, but over the basics of creation. Rav's opinion, that woman was created from Adam's second face, was already alluded to by Rabbi Jeremiah and his account of Adam being created with two faces. But countering that, Samuel doesn't say that Eve was simply created from a rib—no, she was created from a tail!

Why?

Clearly, the head is an emotionally-laden body part—so the Talmud considers that perhaps the opposite body part is appropriate to create woman. Not the top, but the bottom. (It doesn't hurt that the fable also explains why humans, unlike most animals, lack a tail).

So we see, where Klinghoffer wants to use the story of Adam and Eve to put Eve's daughters in one particular box, the Talmud wants to tinker with all the possibilities.

Torah and Divorce

David Klinghoffer isn't happy with the turn that American divorce laws have taken. Here's what he has to say on the topic:

> Secular liberalism insists it only wants to 'free' women— and men too. Besides providing birth control and encouraging women to leave their children with caretakers and join the workforce, it would deregulate marriage altogether. That sounds like a trumpet call for liberty. Indeed, the deregulation of marriage is almost complete. A turning point was in 1969 when California became the first state to allow 'no fault' divorce, meaning that either spouse could terminate a marriage at will without having to produce evidence of immoral or abusive acts by the other spouse. By the mid-1980s, every other state in the union had followed suit. The discourse of liberalism on marriage is replete with words like 'autonomy,' 'self-fulfillment,' and 'choice.' Implicitly, it teaches that society has no stake in the institution of marriage. Partners should be free to come and go from the relationship as they please.[2]

He admits, though, that Judaism is more lenient than he in allowing divorce, and the New Testament even stricter. How fine of him, to be the hyphen in the Judeo-Christian hybrid!

If he would only read the Talmudic law on divorce, he would see

---

[2]   p.33-34

that his "compromise" with Christianity places himself in disagreement with some leading rabbis:

> The School of Shammai said: A man should not divorce his wife unless he has found her guilty of some unseemly conduct, as it says, "because he has found some *unseemly thing* in her."
> The School of Hillel, however, said [that he may divorce her] even if she has merely spoiled his food, since it says, "because *he* has found some unseemly thing in her."
> Rabbi Akiba said, [he may divorce her] even if he finds another woman more beautiful than she is, as it says, "it comes to pass, if she find no favour in his eyes."

It seems like no-fault divorce has the thumbs up from no less an authority than Rabbi Akiba, the foremost Torah sage (and martyr) of the second century.

Klinghoffer tries to weasel out of the contradiction between his personal view on divorce and that of Judaism. He insists that for him,

> what's imperative is... merely to point out that women's natural power base is in the home, not in the office, the legislature, or the governmental executive's mansion, and that a wise society seeks to protect her power.[3]

I've got to say, though, that the Bible sure has odd ways to protect the power of women, certainly when it comes to divorce:

> When a man has taken a wife, and married her, and

---

[3] Klinghoffer, p.35.

it comes to pass that she finds no favor in his eyes, because he has found some uncleanness in her; then let
him write her a bill of divorcement, and give it in her
hand, and send her out of his house. And when she has
departed out of his house, she may go and be another
man's wife. [Deut. 24:1-2]

The Talmud takes this at face value: Without a man's consent, there
is no divorce. And if he wants a divorce and his wife doesn't? He can
still divorce her.

Now, here comes a problem for Jews like Klinghoffer who want to
look to the Torah for absolute "values." One might plausibly argue from
the Jewish laws of divorce that the Torah wants to teach us something
about men and women. I don't really want to guess what it might be
in the nature of men and women that would give only men the key to
enter and end a marital relationship—but I'm sure Klinghoffer would
have some patronizing suggestions.

No, Klinghoffer's problem is that a thousand years ago—which is to
say, two thousand years after the giving of the Torah and five hundred
years after the Talmud—Rabbenu Gershom (the pre-eminent German
rabbi a thousand years ago) decreed that Jewish law would hereafter
require the consent of the woman before allowing divorce.

So who's right?

David Klinghoffer, who would rationalize and rhapsodize the principles of Leviticus as a guide for public policy?

Or Rabbenu Gershom, who took the principles of equity and fair-
ness and made *them* the guide for public policy and adjudicating Jewish
law?

No doubt Rabbenu Gershom outraged the Bible-thumping conservatives of his time, just as Klinghoffer is outraged by America's no-fault
divorce laws, laws which take the Bible's "divorce at will" doctrine and
apply it equally to both sexes. Even accounting for Klinghoffer's love
for Eisenhower's America (or more likely, given his *National Review*
affiliation, to Joe McCarthy's America), it's odd for a moralist—who

calls himself an Orthodox Jew—to admire a system of divorce which encouraged couples to perjure themselves in order to end a marriage, as commonly happened when the state refused to divorce absent proof of adultery.

The bottom line for Orthodox Jews is that divorce is allowable. And unfortunately for bible-thumpers, it exists in the Torah. Divorce also ensures that marriages that persist in this climate are happier, since spouses can leave if they choose to.[4]

So, is Klinghoffer being more righteous than God? The two of them clearly seem at odds on this issue.

Contra Contraception

Klinghoffer believes contraceptives "disempower" a woman by shrinking her domain—the home. On its own, it's a fascinating idea, with intriguing ramifications. Why then the failure of women to object to this disempowerment even while objecting to disempowerment in other spheres? One must assume, if Klinghoffer is correct, that all these women manifest what Marxists call "false consciousness," a handy theory by which one can ignore all evidence which doesn't fit one's ideology.

Don't believe those women who say they want fewer children. Klinghoffer knows what they "really" want. (It's rant like that which leads to date rape).

It's also worth taking a minute to contemplate the brave scope of Klinghoffer's biblical American government. In deciding that contra-

---

4   According to an article by economists Justin Wolfers of Stanford University and Betsey Stevenson of the University of Pennsylvania, in states that relaxed their divorce laws some very good things happened: Fewer women committed suicide, and fewer were murdered by husbands or other "intimate" partners. In addition, both men and women suffered less domestic violence, compared to states that didn't change their laws. In no-fault states, there was a 10 percent drop in a woman's chance of being killed by her spouse or boyfriend. The rate of female suicide in new no-fault states fell by about 20 percent. The effect was more dramatic still for domestic violence—which declined by somewhere between a quarter and a half between 1976 and 1985 in those states that reformed their divorce laws. See http://reason.com/news/show/128136.html for more details.

ception is bad for us, Klinghoffer—who talks of freedom and "moral choices"—doesn't only want to undo a Supreme Court ruling (Griswold v. Connecticut) from the decade before he was born which legalized birth control because of a "right to marital privacy." He wants to second-guess our most intimate decisions.

Such as: Am I going to have sex with my wife tonight? That is, Klinghoffer does not want me to have sex unless my wife is willing to take her chance with getting pregnant. This gives Klinghoffer and the contraception capos a disgusting amount of power over my sex life —and yours too, make no mistake.

Truth be told, I take contraception (as defined by Jewish law) for granted. As did my parents. And as did, for that matter–or so I assume, based on family size–my grandparents.

Klinghoffer would undo the past century... because he deeply knows and understands who my grandmothers really were. He knows the essence of womanhood better than they did. And he knows this how?

Ideology. Conservative ideology.

Because it sure isn't Jewish ideology.

Judaism and Birth Control

To see why I say it isn't a Jewish ideology, let's take a quick look at the discussion of contraception in Jewish law.[5]

In a 100 page discussion of traditional Jewish attitudes toward birth controls, two topics come up. One is "destroying seed." The other is the obligation to "be fruitful and multiply."

Let's look at the second issue first. According to Jewish tradition, this obligation applies only to men.

The rabbis decided that having two children fulfils the double obligation of "be fruitful" and "multiply"

The dominant position is that women *may* use birth control.

---

[5]   For a serious look at these issues, I refer you to the magisterial volume this section is derived from, *Birth Control in Jewish Law: Marital Relations, Contraception, and Abortion As Set Forth in the Classic Texts of Jewish Law* by David M. Feldman, 1968.

In saying that birth control "disempowers" women, Klinghoffer is not quoting the Bible or the Talmud; he is just making something up out of thin air.

Or maybe not. Klinghoffer may be cribbing from Christian theology, which has a far more negative position toward contraception than Judaism, just as it has a far more negative attitude toward sex.

For many Christian thinkers, it is tragic enough that sex is required to make babies. To have sex without the possibility of making babies— God forbid!

This difference between Judaism and Christianity can be seen in the case of a pregnant woman.

Christian theologians urged men to imitate beasts who "once they know the womb is filled... no longer indulge in intercourse or the wantonness of love."[6]

Rabbinic thinkers debated whether a woman was obligated or not to use contraception for the protection of her fetus.

(Incidentally, disputes of this sort are one reason that people knowledgeable about the history of Judaism disdain the term "Judeo-Christian tradition." Ever since Christians went their own way from Judaism, the traditions have diverged. Klinghoffer consistently conflates his personal alliance with Christians against his bogeyman of secular liberals with a real Judeo-Christian tradition, which over the long haul, alas, largely consisted of Christians killing, raping and expelling Judeos.)

Judaism Says No to Saying No

We can see the Christian influence in Klinghoffer's discussion of abortion, when he writes that:

> a purely pro-choice view conforms to the coun-
> terscriptural worldview that I have been developing
> throughout this book, that sees men and women as en-
> trapped in nature, not fully free to resist the demands
> of the body. Abortion as birth control can represent

---

[6]   Feldman, p.181

> an implicit claim by the woman that she couldn't help
> herself, couldn't say no to a desired sexual coupling.[7]

Reread that last second. It's an implicit claim by Klinghoffer that a woman *should* say no to a sexual coupling unless she wants it to result in a baby. Once again, what seems to be a discussion about abortion is actually about the evils of birth control, or rather, the evil of sex.

Again, this is a Christian approach that sees abstinence as a proper way to live, even within a marriage. Judaism is comfortable with sex, and seeks to remove impediments from married couples enjoyment of it.

The anti-sex approach Christian attitudes reached wider in America than just bans on birth control. How else to explain the fact that all fifty states had laws against *heterosexual* sodomy until Illinois became the first to change its law in 1961? Or the fact that in 2003, eight states still had laws on the books which made married couple criminals if they put their bodily parts in the "wrong" places?

What are we to make of such laws, knowing that their repeal is a response to the "secular liberalism" and Constitutional right to privacy that Klinghoffer disdains?

Better yet, what would *God* make of such laws?

As a Jew trying to make sense of God's will, I note a few things.

I note that there is no prohibition of heterosexual sodomy in the Torah.

I note that the *halacha* is clear: "A man can do as he wills with his wife." (Talmud Nedarim 20b) "Unusual" sexual intercourse is therefore explicitly permitted by most authorities.

Further, Judaism mandates that a husband give his wife sexual pleasure.

It's no small matter, therefore, to say: *Whose* God voted for America's sodomy laws?

Certainly not my Jewish God.

My ability to be both a law-abiding American, and a dutiful Jewish

---

[7] Klinghoffer, p.66.

husband, has, on occasion, been the direct result of liberal legislation and jurisprudence. Under the laws of New Jersey thirty years ago, I would be a criminal.

That's why I can't take the "pro-family" rhetoric of Christian conservatives (and their Jewish fellow travelers such as Klinghoffer) too seriously. I don't see any good for my family in allowing the government to regulate my intimate relationship with my wife.

Then again, if I were truly convinced that God didn't want me or my wife to enjoy sex, I'd probably be a cranky, smarmy bastard too. Blessed is God who did not make me a Christian.

Public Affairs?

Klinghoffer explains why the government should be in the marriage regulation business:

> Marriage is institutionalized sexuality. Sexuality is very much a public concern. That is why the biblical commandment of circumcising infant boys (Leviticus 12:3) is carried out, by tradition, in daylight and in public, with a communal audience.[8]

That's funny. When I celebrated the circumcision of my son, I plumb forgot to invite the governor, the mayor and the chief of police. Except for the *mohel* who performed the ceremony, it was a strictly friends and family affair.

In fact, a *bris*, a circumcision ceremony, is considered a celebration for the entire Jewish people. Not because we're all watching over the sex life of an eight-day-old baby (ewww!), but because we're welcoming a newcomer into the tribe. The public concern and celebration is about fecundity, not sexuality. Klinghoffer's conflation of the two bespeaks a mind that is either Christian or filthy, or both.

Which is not to say that circumcisions are never governmental mat-

[8] Klinghoffer, p.34.

ters. The Syrian-Greek King Antiochus banned circumcisions. So did the Romans. The lesson of Jewish history is that governments are not to be trusted—and that it can be very relaxing to have a public event without involving the authorities.

Are our weddings and divorces really public affairs? There's no indication from the Bible that this is the case. The Torah mandates no registrar to hand out marriage licenses.

Or is a marriage really a private matter? Should a wedding simply be —as the Bible says—"when a man takes a woman"? The answer to that question—from a Jewish standpoint—undermines the entire premise of Klinghoffer's book.

Where Klinghoffer would read the Bible to extract values to impose on society, the Talmudic sages felt free—even compelled—to modify Biblical rules for the good of society.

And marriage and divorce were at the center of their efforts to improve the workings of societies.

It was here that they created the central institutions of Jewish marriage: the wedding blessings under the wedding canopy, carried out before witnesses and an assembly of at least ten people.

In fact, the actual institution of marriage is of such little importance for the Bible that the Hebrew word for marriage does not pre-date Rabbinic Hebrew. According to the authoritative four-volume *Even Shoshan* Hebrew dictionary, all the cognate words for *nisuin*—words meaning married, marriage, to marry—all these are of Rabbinic Hebrew, developed long after the time of the Bible. In the time of the Bible—linguistically speaking—there was no marriage or wedding; there was only bride and groom, man and woman, "taking" and "sending out."

And there is another aspect of Biblical marriages that was basically ignored by the rabbis of the Talmud, and finally overturned altogether by the post-Talmudic rabbis.

I refer to polygamy, the arrangement by which our father Abraham also took his wife's servant Hagar as a concubine, and by which our father Jacob married both Rachel *and* Leah.

In perhaps a hint by God that the nature of relationships not only could evolve, but *should* evolve, the Torah, in a later book of the Pentateuch, explicitly bans a man from marrying two sisters. Jacob's marriages are not, by the Torah's standards, kosher.

This evolution of family standards and values towards a more equal and egalitarian relationship stretches from the patriarchs in Genesis, to the law of the Torah at Sinai, through the developments we have seen in Talmudic and later times. The process of change we see in the Torah itself points toward a process of evolution, though one that's easy to miss, accustomed as we are to taking our own personal family structures for granted and imagining the selfsame types reflected in earlier teachings. We generally don't notice this evolution within the Torah, and we certainly don't notice the difference between the Bible's families and our own, so steeped are we in our own families.

So, for example, Rabbi Dr. Norman Lamm, chancellor of Yeshiva University, equates polygamy with incest, bestiality and necrophilia[9]– apparently forgetting, in the heat of passionate rhetoric, that polygamy is respected in the Torah, and not banned. Moreover, Israel's 12 sons were the products of four simultaneous wives. At its root, this is a failure of imagination: Lamm cannot imagine that Jacob was not a cultured Manhattan Orthodox Jew.

Imagining a Golden Age

A similar failure of imagination occurs with Klinghoffer's apparent desire for a golden age of stronger, more secure and better families. He cannot imagine that America endured eras with higher jumps in divorce rates, and rates of teenage pregnancy and pregnant brides than we do today. He worries about a breakdown of some golden age-old ideal

---

[9]   The Jew And The Gentile, The Commentator, 1/28/08 (http://media.www. yucommentator.com/media/storage/paper652/news/2008/01/28/Features/The-Jew. And.The.Gentile-3169652.shtml)

Necrophilia is not specifically banned by the Torah, though it is clearly at odds with the Rabbinic notions of respecting the dead. Lamm, here, like Klinghoffer, ignores the fact that liberal ethics based on personhood and consent can suppress bestiality, necrophilia, and most incest.

of the American family, which he fears gay marriage will accelerate.

But just as Jewish marriage has changed over the millennia from polygamous to monogamous, so has the American marriage changed over the centuries and decades.

Gay marriage, says Klinghoffer, "is a symptom that deepens the underlying illness" of American marriage. "Gay marriage may be compared to a broken window on a city street. Civilization itself is fragile."

Klinghoffer quotes Professor Stephanie Coontz on the state of contemporary American marriage, that as a social ideal "it has become optional and more brittle" and that "the number of unmarried couples living together in the United States increased sevenfold" between the 1970s and 1999. He agrees with Coontz that the push for gay marriage is "an inevitable result of the previous revolution in heterosexual marriage."

But though he quotes Coontz, he completely misses the point of her book, *Marriage, A History: How Love Conquered Marriage*. Coontz disagrees with Klinghoffer strongly when it comes to diagnosing the ills of marriage and prescribing policy solutions.

As Coontz summarizes[10]:

> Some of the tremendous problems we face in modern American society—from drug use to economic instability to personal alienation—have developed in conjunction with a series of remarkable changes in the composition and functioning of American families, and many people link these two sets of facts. They blame the problems on changes in family roles or val-

---

10   "In Search Of A Golden Age: A look at families throughout U.S. history reveals there has never been an 'ideal form'" by Stephanie Coontz in *Caring For Families* (IC#21) Spring 1989, Page 18 http://www.context.org/ICLIB/IC21/Coontz.htm retrieved June 15, 2008]

ues and argue that a return to some "traditional" or "natural" family would resolve the crisis.

My research suggests that all the historical evidence contradicts such a conclusion. On closer inspection, no "golden age" of the family can be found, and many of our ideals are based on a mythical family that never existed in the real world. The source of many of America's modern problems, moreover, both in and outside of the family, does not lie in a departure from old family practices and values but in the clash between unrealistic expectations and a changing socioeconomic environment. The real crisis of American society is over how to handle the dependencies associated not only with infancy and age but with illness, unemployment, and degradation of the environment. Solving the crisis will require social commitments and obligations that extend beyond the nuclear family.

As she further says,

I've argued, then, that "common sense" causal arguments suggesting that deviant families are the cause of many social problems do not hold water. Such misconceptions stem from the idea that there is some natural family form out there, whose relationships are somehow "better" for people's development than other families. Of course we know that some relationships have a healthy dynamic in our society and some don't, but that's a very different thing from saying that one particular form is most likely to create healthy relationships and should therefore be imposed on people, regardless of their diverse conditions. As adaptable and flexible institutions that operate in the real world, families are constantly changing. They cannot be constructed (or deconstructed) on ideological grounds.

Perhaps the most important implication of this argument for policymaking is that we should avoid simplistic value judgments about family relationships. The astonishing variety of structures that people have used to coordinate reproduction and organize emotional interactions suggests that any solutions we attempt should not rest on blaming the family or setting up restrictive definitions of what a proper family is. We need to recognize the fluidity of family boundaries under different social and economic settings, respect the ways that people improvise in order to survive, and seek ways of supporting their own decisions and actions rather than trying to force them to accept models of what a family should be that do not exist in history and are ideological in nature.

Coontz traces several distinct family structures in American history. For those looking to the Bible for family advice, hers is a useful reminder that what binds together our families today—the family we grew up in, the family we form as adults—may be far different than what bound together families in Biblical times.

Biblical Bureaucrats in the Bedroom

Klinghoffer is similarly parochial as he glibly dismisses the possibility of a real theocracy, in full bureaucratic seriousness, crouching at the door.

But make no mistake: While Klinghoffer avers that he has no desire for theocracy, in the real world of 21st century earth, a theocratic bureaucracy imposing religious demands on families isn't just science fiction; it's a real possibility. And not just in the Muslim world.

In the State of Israel, all marriages and divorces are regulated by religious authorities. The Chief Rabbinate oversees weddings and divorces for Jews; similar bodies register personal status for Christians and Muslims.

An Israeli Jews who wishes to marry a non-Jew is strictly out of luck. The couple can't get married in their native land.

That's the treatment gays now face in most of America.

But if we're to go down the Israeli path of legislating marriage licenses in line with Leviticus, we can't let menses go unmentioned.

The Torah is very strict about this: A man should not have sex with a menstruating woman. (Funny how conservatives never talk about Biblical restrictions on *heterosexuals*. What is it with their gay obsession, I wonder?)

Now, I'm not going to mock the laws of *nidah*, as the rules of menstruating women are known, if only because I observe them. Just as God tells me I can eat some foods and not others, work some days and not others, so too can my wife and I have sex some days and not others. (Besides its religious value, forced abstinence has in its favor that—like beating one's head against the wall—it feels so good when it stops.)

Now, you might argue that sex during menstruation is private, whereas a marriage license is public. That would be a sensible point. However, the Israeli rabbinate has little truck for the sensible, preferring, in true theocratic spirit, to be limited only by the possible. They can't enforce the laws of *nidah* during the marriage. But they can, and do, insist that every Jewish bride dip in a ritual bath before her wedding. And they also insist that the wedding not be scheduled for a day when the bride menstruating.[411]

So you see, applying Biblical values to marriages really *is* possible.

Klinghoffer's Marriage and Mine

Is it fair to ask: Why is Klinghoffer so worried about other people's marriages? Is his own so shaky?

I have to confess: I didn't get married because I believed in the institution of marriage. I got married because I had found for myself the kindest, smartest, prettiest, funniest woman I could imagine—and I

---

[11] See Yudelson, Larry, "To live together: Israeli rabbinate counsels couples", *Long Island Jewish World*, September 15-21, 1990, p.20

wanted to live with her. Getting married and having a party were just a convenient and fun outer manifestation of our inner state.

Now, I don't know why other men get married. Clearly, they're settling for second best (though if they haven't met my wife, they may be lucky enough not to realize it). But it's seriously sad to think of someone getting married because they think they *should*, because it's the *right* thing to do, rather than because they've found someone they can't see living without.

I know people who married because it seemed the right thing to do... and then divorced when they discovered doing the right thing wasn't enough to make life livable.

That's why gay marriage doesn't bother me. It's not law–secular or religious–that made me marry Eve rather than Steve. If straight marriage were *banned* I'd still choose Eve over Steve.

The fact that some men seem bound to their wives only because their religion tells them they can't pursue the men they really want—well, I feel sad for their wives—and for them. And while I have no idea about Klinghoffer personally, I just have to say—if there's a reason conservatives like Ted Haggard, the disgraced leader of the National Association of Evangelicals discovered to have repeatedly paid for sex with a male prostitute, preach about "family values," they seem to be having a public conversation to convince themselves about the matter. It's too bad the rest of us have to suffer for it.

Klinghoffer wants us to think that the Bible calls for strong families and abhors divorce. Perhaps he is following the Christian mistake of reading New Testament conclusions back into what they call the Old Testament. The New Testament does have verses calling for men to rule over their wives[12] – a sentiment not echoed in earlier Jewish scripture or later Rabbinic teachings. And the New Testament speaks out against

---

[12]   E.g.: "Let the women learn in silence with all subjection. But I suffer not a woman to teach, nor to usurp authority over the man, but to be in silence. For Adam was first formed, then Eve. And Adam was not deceived, but the woman being deceived was in the transgression" (I Tim. 2: 11-14). "Wives, submit yourselves unto your own husbands, as unto the Lord. For the husband is the head of the wife..." (Ephesians 5: 22-23).

divorce, a view Rabbinic jurisprudence rejected. For a Jew in the voting booth, there seems little reason to think of either divorce *or* marriage.

Except.... there is one relevant verse from the Torah that the rabbis thought worth contemplating when thinking of politics. The verse is "Love your neighbor as yourself," and the Talmud (Nidah 17a) applies it to the intimate details of the marital relationship. Clearly, in Judaism, this commandment, which ideally should govern *all* interpersonal relationships, certainly indicates the mutuality and consideration required in a marriage.

How one acts in one's marriage can provide an indication of how one fulfills this important obligation, as well as one's attitude toward God in general.

In this light, a candidate's personal behavior may have ramifications that should be considered when voting. What, then, should Americans make of Senator John McCain? Upon returning from Vietnam, McCain used his celebrity status to meet and socialize with a millionaire beer heiress, ignoring his wife who had been disfigured in an auto accident? What should we say about a political career launched with money gained from an adulterous relationship? Did that reflect someone fulfilling the commandment of "Love your neighbor as yourself?

Am I saying that this should be the deciding factor when casting a ballot? Of course not. Israel's greatest political leader, King David, was also its most famous adulterer (and unlike McCain, he compounded his sin with murder). But by the same token, it seems ridiculous to look to a political party to, by its platform, change the spiritual, societal shape of American families, if its leaders can't even do what's right by their own wives.

5

Marrying for Love, Mating for Life

It seems incredible. Just 40 years after the Stonewall Riots launched the Gay Pride movement, the legal right to marriage has been extended to same-sex couples in two states, with the legal equivalent in several others.

How have societal attitudes changed so fast?

Maybe because the basic argument for equality is so strong.

Even Klinghoffer, writing with the avowed goal of providing "Biblical" wisdom and scriptural rather than political reasoning, has difficulty making a case against gay marriage. As we'll see, he spends a good portion of his ten pages explaining the reasons *in favor* of gay marriage—and while he ultimately dismisses them, we'll see for ourselves that he's actually trafficking in some spectacularly flimsy anti-gay arguments.

Klinghoffer divides religious arguments permitting gay marriage into three groups:

> First of all, some argue that on same-sex relation-
> ships the Bible doesn't mean what it seems to mean.
> Second, others prefer to say that while the passages
> denouncing homosexual practice really do mean what
> they seem to mean, that fact shouldn't deter us from
> accepting the liberal view on the issue. Why? Because
> biblical teaching itself would even mandate that the
> troublesome verse may be disregarded. Third, another
> view admits that the Bible may reject same-sex love,
> but insists that we are justified in dismissing its view
> because nowadays we understand things about sexual-
> ity and society that the scriptural authors did not.[1]

Klinghoffer omits an important fourth argument: Why should secular marriage depend on a Biblical imprimatur? One can imagine situa-
tions (same-sex, or religious intermarriage, or even interracial couples)
in which one cleric might refuse to officiate, but some other religious
figure, or the state, might perform a valid marriage service for the happy couple. Sometimes you just have to find the right vendor.

In general, those of us who keep Biblical commandments do not
take it upon ourselves to force our private observances upon others.
Our practice of our religion is between us and our God. We prefer the
freedom to worship as we see fit, and champion that right for others,
even if they believe differently than we do.

This is one of the reasons that Jews have historically cherished the
separation of Church and State. It has allowed us to be both good
Americans and good Jews. In other countries, at other times, we weren't
always so lucky.

We've already dismissed the claim that same-sex marriage is harm-
ful to society—his response to the third group of pro-gay marriage
arguments. As we saw in the last chapter, that claim was predicated on

---

[1]   Klinghoffer, p.38

an understanding of marriage that reflects neither Biblical nor socio-logical realties.

As for his second set of objections, which would dismiss the biblical prohibition against homosexual acts as inapplicable for American soci-ety, Klinghoffer explains:

> Commenting on the original text in Leviticus, the notorious verse 18:22—"You shall not lie with a man as one lies with a woman, it is an abomination"—Jacob Milgrom points out that it occurs in the context of specifically Jewish legislation. Thus the name of the in-tended recipient of the commandment against homo-sexual intercourse is Jews, not gentiles. Indeed, verse 18:20 warns married couples not to engage in sexual intercourse when the female partner is menstruating, a feature only of Jewish law. [2]

So, these rules apply to Jews alone, and *not* to the greater American populace.

But in basing his opinion on the usage of the word *toevah*, "abomina-tion," which he explains as "designat[ing] a range of morally culpable acts," Klinghoffer makes a telling and unforgivable error, completely ignoring the "ritual," and therefore a-political, nature of many of the "abominations" discussed in the Bible.

The effort to categorize the Torah's commands as ritual or moral laws, (with a claim that *toevah* refers only to the latter) is problematic because the Bible makes no such distinctions between "ritual" or "moral" dicta. A commandment is a commandment is a commandment. The rabbis dealt with problems like these by erasing the differences between the Torah laws, claiming that one could not speak of relative rewards of a small commandment and a greater one. For the rabbis, small laws exact the same meticulous adherence as the bigger, flashier laws.

---

[2]   Klinghoffer, p.42

Leviticus 18:22 is indeed a troubling verse for anyone who bases his religious life on the Bible. But for those of us taking part in the political task of voting for candidates, Klinghoffer's fixation on homosexual acts seems pruriently misplaced. Let's see why.

The Bible categorizes three types of acts as *toevah*, "abomination." (The divisions are my own, based on the various contexts.)

ETHICAL: The Bible prohibits ethical offenses of lying, cheating, and stealing, particularly from widows and orphans.

SEXUAL: A man lying with a man is singled out—twice—as "abomination" but the list in Leviticus 18 concludes with a summary, using the Hebrew plural form, "do not do *any* of these abominations." Included, then, is: bestiality; having a sex with a menstruating woman; having sex with another man's wife; or dallying with a woman and her sister. Another sexual offense specifically singled out as a serious 'abomination' in Deuteronomy 24:4, is the scenario of a woman who divorces her second husband and returns to her first.

Observant Jews consider it hairsplitting for someone to transgress the rules of *nidah*—separation during a woman's menstrual period— yet oppose homosexuality. *Heterosexuals* who practice abominations are in no position to lecture homosexuals. Period.

Rabbinic jurisprudence considers anal intercourse the *only* homosexual act prohibited by the Torah. Whether gay couples commit this act when the lights are out should be shrouded in the same cloak of privacy—and given the same benefit of the doubt—as heterosexual couples who may or may not be observing the laws of *nidah* in *their* bedrooms.

If that is a position among those who take the Torah seriously, what is gained by inviting the secular state to poke its nose in? Why would the state even refer to the Bible at all to decide who it will or will not join in matrimony?

If you really think the government should stamp out abominations— or at least not sanction them—homosexual marriage should be your last concern, not your first.

Why? Because the most commonly violated laws prohibiting *toevah* in the Torah are mentioned in Deuteronomy 14:3. Klinghoffer omits this category entirely, perhaps because it conclusively undermines his entire argument. Here it is:

FOOD: Deuteronomy 14:3 states, "Do not eat any abomination." The passage then proceeds to list which animals are kosher and which are not. The clear message is that the consumption of these non-kosher animals is an abomination.

And yet, the federal government spends money promoting the raising and distribution of pigs, lobster, shrimp and other abominations.

I have no doubt that if you were to total all the Biblical abominations committed on any given Saturday night, transgressions involving non-kosher food and menstrual sex would far outnumber homosexual acts.

So why the fuss about gays?[3]

As Klinghoffer acknowledges, there have been a number of arguments offered as to why the Torah prohibition on male-male sex might simply not apply to committed homosexual marriages:

> Religious liberals insist that we are reading back into the text recent moral precepts that aren't really there. The Bible isn't forbidding homosexual intercourse of a loving, lawful, committed kind like that practiced in Massachusetts. It says nothing about such love! Rather it has in mind certain varieties of sexual exploitation that were cruel, unjust, unloving, and, needless to say, uncommitted. Regarding the Leviticus texts, about men lying "with mankind, as he lieth with a woman," one theory holds that it refers only to forbidden acts of ritual prostitution.

---

[3]   We're omitting from our discussion one verse that is perhaps more central to his argument than Klinghoffer lets on, the New Testament passage in 1 Corinthians 6 in which Paul condemns the "effeminate" and "abusers of themselves with mankind." As a Jew, it's not my place to puzzle out why Paul permits the eating of pork – an abomination—but lumps homosexuals among the "unrighteous [who] shall not inherit the kingdom of God." It seems very convenient and more than a little heartless for Paul and his followers to bash gays with bacon grease dripping from their *own* chins.

Another theory, advanced in the prestigious Anchor Bible commentary series by University of California–Berkeley scholar Jacob Milgrom, says that the Torah only has a problem with homosexual relations because the Bible wishes to keep reproduction and child-rearing within the bounds of a stable family. Why not let a gay couple marry and then adopt children? The sole objection there would be that the Bible doesn't have a concept of adoption. But now that adoption is a well-known and accepted institution, there should be no objection to a gay couple marrying and raising a family: If gay partners adopt children, they do not violate the intent of the prohibition in Leviticus.[4]

After enumerating these theories, Klinghoffer rejects them thusly:

The fact that so many divergent theories have been advanced indicates that something other than dis-interested scholarship is at work. We observe here a mad and desperate dash by various writers, all eagerly seeking to reach the same conclusion—that the Bible's obvious meaning isn't its true meaning—but none in their collective haste being especially careful about how they get there. [5]

Excuse me? Is that the best you can do?

As we explained in our opening chapters, rabbinic Judaism *always* brings two or three opinions. Jews expect it. It's no surprise that con-temporary commentators follow this tradition.

By this logic, the fact that there might well be three reasons to vote for John McCain means that none of them are true.

If you don't find this legerdemain plausible, then, congratulations:

---

[4]   Klinghoffer, p.39
[5]   Klinghoffer, p.40

Klinghoffer has proven that gay marriage should not only be allowed by your state legislator, but by your house of worship as well.

If, on the other hand, you believe Klinghoffer is right when he claims that too many proofs spoil the broth, you'll be relieved to hear that I am going to offer yet another reading of Jewish texts that will argue that homosexual marriage is not what Leviticus 18 is talking about.

I will start by reading an unusual and memorable passage from the Talmud. In the process, I will take out a few of Klinghoffer's remaining arguments against gay marriage.

Let us begin by looking in Genesis, at the creation of Eve:

> And the Lord God said, It is not good that the man should be alone; I will make him a help to match him. And out of the ground the Lord God formed every beast of the field, and every bird of the air; and brought them to Adam to see what he would call them; and whatever Adam called every living creature, that was its name. And Adam gave names to all cattle, and to the bird of the air, and to every beast of the field; but for Adam there was not found a help to match him. [Gen 2:18-20]

The verse "it is not good that man should be alone" is famous. But why does God follow up on this observation by trotting all the living creatures before Adam to have them named?

The Talmud finds the answer in Genesis 2:23, in a verse immediately after Eve is formed:

> "And Adam said, *This* is now bone of my bones and flesh of my flesh."

Explains Rabbi Eleazar:

> "This teaches that Adam had intercourse with every

beast and animal but found no satisfaction until he co-habited with Eve." [Talmud Yebamot 63a]

In other words, Adam did more than just meet, greet and name the beasts.

And that may be more than you wanted to know about our first biblical ancestor.

Properly understood, though, this Midrash is telling us something essential about a helpmate, a spouse.

One imagines, given the reports of farm boys dating their animals, that any female genitalia, regardless of their trappings, are capable of doing their job. Adam presumably found several similarly satisfying matches in the Eden menagerie.

What he didn't find, what he couldn't find, was a true helpmeet—an equal, a peer, a partner. Adam couldn't find love.

It is clear that God the matchmaker wants something more for Adam than a sex partner; God wants him to have a complete partnership.

It is of interest to note that the Hebrew phrase for what God seeks for Adam—*ezer k'negdo*, a "help to match him"—is written using the male gender. (Hebrew is a gendered language. The feminine form of that phrase would read *"ezrah k'negdo."*) It as if God is saying that what is important is the helper, not the helper's sex.

We can now turn to the passage that Klinghoffer sees as his conclusive argument, the ancient Rabbinic commentary, the Sifra on Leviticus 18:25, which condemns the Canaanites for marrying men to men.

Rabbi Brad Artson addressed this Sifra text back in 1990.

> Rabbi David Novak suggests a parallel from Suetonius (Lives of the Caesars 4.28), where that author mentions that the Roman Emperor Nero gave a marriage contract to a few of his favorite male sex partners. Clearly that kind of "marriage"—to one of his many objects of lust of both sexes—is a far cry from a loving, supportive, or sacred relationship. In that

context, the passage from Sifra speaks to the same issue as other passages—claiming the appearance of sanctity and commitment for loveless expressions of lust. It is more reasonable to read the Sifra in the context of its time than in that of our own.[6]

The Sifra, then, is speaking about homosexual liaisons along the line of Adam's flings with the wild kingdom. Such a scenario would have no bearing on the intentions of loving, committed, contemporary gay couples seeking a marriage license.

What I find most convincing about this line of reasoning is that it accounts for the placement of the prohibition on homosexual acts within the rubric of Leviticus 18.

Klinghoffer points to its place following the prohibition of "giving children to Moloch" for his best and final excuse for denying high-profile gay journalist Andrew Sullivan the right to joint health insurance with his husband. Unfortunately, the very nature of "giving children to Moloch" is lost in the mists of history; Klinghoffer uses it for a mostly circular argument about how gay marriage undermines marriage and hurts children. Surprise, surprise.

Let me offer a more serious answer to the question, one that ignores the amorphous Moloch prohibition but looks at following verse. Why is the prohibition on homosexual sex in Leviticus followed by the prohibition against bestiality?

According to my theory, it is precisely sex with animals that the Bible wants us to avoid. *This* is the abomination. The Torah is banning Adam and *sheep*, not Adam and Steve.

By the same token, the Torah may well actually prefer a committed homosexual relationship to the prospect of heterosexual flings with prostitutes or beer heiresses. Such flings, particularly when conducted by married men, certainly undermine the institution of marriage more than homosexual marriage ever could.

---

[6]   Bradley S. Artson, "Gay and Lesbian Jews: A Teshuvah," *Jewish Spectator*, Winter 1990.

6

Klinghoffer's Abortion Distortion

Having read the chapter titled: *Abortion: A Litmus Test,* I must say that Klinghoffer is a decent writer, and he manages to do a lot with the scant support in scripture for his position.

So I sat down and put together a reasonable response to Klinghoffer's argument on how God votes on the abortion issue. But before I get there, I must share with you what Joseph Farah had to say about the book.

Joseph Farah is one of those Internet commentators whose diatribes your right-winger neighbor in shul is likely to send you until you threaten to filter out his emails. It was therefore a pleasure to read Farah's disappointment in Klinghoffer's effort:

> If that is a "conservative" agenda, I'm glad I am not
> a "conservative" but rather an independent-minded

American faithful to the U.S. Constitution and guided by his own understanding of God's Word.
[WorldNetDaily.com, June 4, 2008]

Farah is a pro-Israel Lebanese-American, and his attack is purely ideological and cannot be blamed on anti-Jewish sentiment. The fact that I can't stand his writing doesn't make it invalid. Millions of Christians and Jews adore him (see paragraph 3).

But Farah's attack exposes the fundamental problem in Klinghoffer's methodology, as he tries to pawn off a rabbinical approach to Torah text on a wide public that has no recognition of its roots nor its validity. Throughout the chapter, Klinghoffer mixes Biblical citations (accepted by Jews *and* Christians) with rabbinical citations (accepted *only* by Jews, and even then not all of us, really). It has to be a losing effort when it comes to fundamentalist Bible thumpers like Joseph Farah.

I actually loved Farah's taunt of Klinghoffer the Conservative wannabe, specifically on the abortion chapter. Farah writes:

> Here's how I believe God would have us vote on [abortion]—and why: …There are many familiar passages of Scripture that have been used to show that killing unborn children, the most innocent of life, is not God's way: Psalm 94:21, Ecclesiastes 11:5, Isaiah 59:7, Genesis 42:22, Proverbs 28:13, Deuteronomy 21:9, Psalm 139:13-16 and Luke 1:41-47 to name a few. But to make this simple, every time the Bible refers to a pregnant woman, it says she is "with child." We don't talk like that any more in our 21st century American culture because we don't want to acknowledge the child until the day it is born—if it is allowed to be born. But check out how often the Bible refers to women "with child": Genesis 16:4, Genesis 19:36, Genesis 38:24, Exodus 21:22, 1 Samuel 4:19, 2 Samuel 11:5, 2 Kings 8:12, Isaiah 26:17, Mathew 1:18, Mathew 1:23, Luke

2:5, 1 Thessalonians 5:3 and Revelation 12:2.

I don't know from Revelation, Matthew, or Luke, but I did look up Farah's citations from the Jewish Bible, which are way more extensive than Klinghoffer's, but are about as credible about abortion as the evangelical proof that Jesus is mentioned in Jewish scripture. Total rubbish.

☞   Psalm 94:21—*"They gang up against the soul of the righteous, and condemn the blood of the innocent."* The psalm is about how God will punish the wicked some day soon. How the verse is more about the killing of fetuses than about any other innocent person I fail to understand.

☞   Ecclesiastics 11:5—*"Just as you do not know the way of the spirit or the bones in the pregnant belly, likewise you do not comprehend the works of God who makes everything."* And how is this a prohibition against abortion? Sheer nonsense.

☞   Isaiah 59:7—*"Their feet run to evil, and they make haste to shed innocent blood, their thoughts are thoughts of iniquity; wasting and destruction are in their paths."* A pattern emerges: Every time Farah spots innocent blood, it's gotta' be a fetus. Interesting idea, especially when juxtaposed with the Christian idea of Original Sin, which suggests them fetuses is full of sin like the worst among us, un-saved folks...

Anyway, so Farah employs the evangelical tradition of raping the Biblical text until it gives up the ghost. I mean, he even brings Genesis 42:22, where Reuven cautions his brothers not to kill the child, as if the sons of Jacob were in the middle of an anti-abortion rally (the child in question is, of course, Joseph, who was 17 at the time, a story Farah should know, as he shares a first name with the lad).

The reason I've digressed so much with the Farah citations is to show what happens when you just roam in the scriptural text, picking verses that seem to fit your opinion. If, on top of it, you're working from a translation of the Hebrew, you're very likely to stray in both comical *and* tragic fashion.

Unlike Farah, Klinghoffer is, ostensibly, bound by rabbinical tradition, which scorns that kind of unsubstantiated cherry picking, because the latter often yields grossly inedible cherries. So Klinghoffer's search of legitimate Biblical comments on abortion ends up with this begrudging admission:

> A liberal Bible interpreter, meanwhile, could confront us with the most troubling passage for the pro-life cause, Exodus 21:22-25, which has the merit of being a legal text.[1]

You know something? Whether you're a liberal interpreter or a troubled pro-lifer, why not read the verse as is? By the way, the strictly abortion-related verses are only Exodus 21:22-23:

> If men fight, and hurt a pregnant woman, so that her children exit her, and yet no tragedy follows, they shall be surely punished, according to what the woman's husband will lay upon them, as determined by a judge. And if tragedy follows, then you shall exact a life for a life.

Klinghoffer stops short of taking the text to its logical conclusion, but, supposedly because he's no liberal interpreter, would not declare the obvious *kal vachomer*[2] here: If when you hit a woman accidentally and she loses her fetus you're not a murderer, then of course if you extract her fetus with her consent you're certainly not a murderer.

There's no other conclusion from this passage vis-à-vis the legality of a doctor performing an abortion.

---

[1] Klinghoffer, p.60.

[2] That's *a fortiori,* for those of you who prefer your major-to-minor arguments described in Latin rather than Hebrew.

If he does it without consent he pays damages, if he does it *with* consent he probably should get paid for his trouble.

Now, the fact that the Torah does not call for the execution of abortion doctors does not mean that it promotes the use of abortion, most certainly not as a means of birth control. I do agree, then, with Klinghoffer's assertion:

> Though liberal Jewish groups, I'm sorry to say, like to cover this up, the rabbis of the Talmud, contemplating America in the opening decade of the twenty-first century, would say the hundreds of thousands of such murders are being committed by Americans against unborn babies every year.[3]

I'm not so sure the rabbis of the Talmud would be describing abortions as murder even if they were suddenly resurrected in our time, but without a doubt they would have frowned on such a widespread practice. But the rabbis probably would also have differentiated the relative value of gentile and Jewish fetuses.

I'm not sure how they would have dealt with the notion of "pro-choice," which presupposes a woman's ownership of her body. Intuitively, I would have assumed that the value of life and the duty of preserving life are so paramount, they supersede the claim of self-ownership. Yet the Talmud is not explicit on the prohibition of suicide, which is another example of executing self-ownership. Our rabbinical strict anti-suicide decisions are post-Talmudic. In fact, the Talmud entertains cases in which suicide is not only permitted but encouraged (*yehareg u'bal ya'avor*).

Of course, sanctioned suicide is not the same as suicide by choice. Rather, these are cases of suicide for the sake of avoiding the transgression of one of the three superior laws (blasphemy, murder, and illicit sex), which could be interpreted to mean that we do *not* own our bod-

---

[3] Klinghoffer, p.61.

ies, since on some rare occasions we are obligated to relinquish them.

But an examination of later authors on this question of necessary suicide (or permitting oneself to be killed)—most explicitly in Maimonides' *Igeret HaShmad*—reveals a reluctance to demand of Jews to be martyred rather than be forcibly converted (blasphemy). Maimonides states that one who does not rise to the challenge of martyrdom, and abandons Judaism under duress, is not considered an apostate and does not deserve any degradation or punishment.

So perhaps it can be said that Maimonides does offer tacit recognition of a personal choice regarding the preservation of one's life when faced with defilement through a super-transgression.

All of which spells bad news for Klinghoffer, whose agenda, to remind you, is turning God into a card-carrying conservative.

So Klinghoffer picks Genesis 9:6 to try and promote his cause. On its face, the verse is as abortion-related as those Jospeh Farah quotes:

> He who sheds man's blood, by man shall his blood
> be shed, for in the image of God made He man.

Klinghoffer brings a Talmudic citation from Rabbi Yishmael, which offers a different punctuation: *He who sheds a person's blood* inside *a person—his blood be shed*. So we should extend the death penalty even to those who kill a fetus, which is the only "person inside a person."

The problem with citing a single argument out of a huge, multi-page Talmudic discussion of the death penalty, is that it deprives the reader of an awareness of the numerous other arguments which do not make this point, and also of an appreciation of how minute this opinion is within the flow of the discussion. It also obscures the fact that the discussion is of the death penalty for gentiles, and that Rabbi Yishmael's opinion concerns only a gentile who performs an abortion.

One thing is for certain – there is no suggestion, not even a hint, that the sages considered abortion a capital offense. As Menachem Elon— who authored the *Encyclopedia Judaica* article which Klinghoffer relies

on extensively in this chapter—put it: "Thus abortion, although prohibited, does not constitute murder (Tos., Sanh. 59a; Hul. 33a)."

A bit later it's a pleasure watching Klinghoffer trying to sell the rabbinical concept of the fetus being considered viable only after 40 days
in the womb. But one loses one's benign tendencies after reading the
entire chapter and realizing the author has dealt with a whole bunch of
esoteric stuff, even mixed in a citation from Paul John II, but neglected
to discuss the central rabbinical argument *in favor* of abortion.

The basic Talmudic priorities regarding a conflict between the life of
the mother and that of the fetus are delineated by Rashi on Sanhedrin
72b:

> Regarding a woman having a difficult birth which
> threatens her life, the midwife may insert her hand and
> cut up the fetus and extract it in pieces, because as long
> as it hasn't come out into the world it is not considered
> a living being and one may kill it to save its mother.

This is the core of our belief in the rabbinical permission to perform
abortions. Not because the fetus isn't a viable person until the 40th day
of gestation, but because it is not viable until the *very end* of gestation.
When it has taken its first breath it has become equal to its mother, two
living human beings each with the right to life. Until it has completed
its exit from the womb, even if it is stuck halfway, as long as it hasn't
taken a breath it's still part of Mommy, and, sadly, we would terminate
its life to save Mommy's.

In other words, not only do the Rabbis permit late-term abortion,
they actually base their entire understanding of the legal relationship
between mother and fetus on the late-term conflict between those two
lives, one which is fully realized and one which is still only potential.
And in rabbinical law we always go with the life we have, not the life
that might appear in the future.

Klinghoffer's most serious offense against the reader is not the cherry
picking and the quoting out of context, which are the tools of his trade.
It is his intentional deletion of the most important rabbinical ruling

concerning the rights of a pregnant woman: She is superior to her fetus and may choose to terminate its life in extreme cases.

How would God vote, then, pro-choice or pro-life? Pro-choice, with the obvious proviso that abortions must only be used as a last resort. God would very likely avoid the pro-life candidate whose position deprives women of their essential rights.

7

You Say You Don't Want Evolution

And now we come to the "Big E"—evolution. Klinghoffer titles his chapter "Education: If God Ran for School Board," but after briefly reciting the history of Jewish communal education, he moves on to his central agenda: allowing schools to teach "the scientific controversy around Darwin's theory" of evolution.

This is Klinghoffer's day job. He is a fellow at the Discovery Institute, which has been leading the effort to repackage anti-evolutionary creationism as anti-Darwinian "intelligent design."

For me this chapter is personal; it was the subject of my first dust-up with Klinghoffer. In 2006, Klinghoffer wrote an op-ed, "Darwin's Jews" that appeared in the *New York Jewish Week*. I responded with an essay entitled "Darwin is Not the Enemy." My work elicited Klinghoffer's reply, "Darwin is a problem for Jews," which appeared in the *Jerusalem Post*. I'll draw upon my essay, and respond to some of Klinghoffer's later points, in this discussion.

Raising the personal stakes even higher, this chapter contains one of Klinghoffer's most daring insults toward his ideological opponents.[1] Here he singles out religious believers like myself who see no conflict between our religious faith and our embrace of evolutionary science. One who believes in God and accepts evolution, says Klinghoffer, is akin to the Israelites berated by the prophet Elijah for believing in both Baal and God: "How long will you dance between opinions?" Klinghoffer quotes the Book of Kings, "If the Lord is the God, go after Him! And if the Baal, go after it!"

So: Accepting evolutionary biology is the same as worshiping Baal?

Not according to Rabbi Abraham Isaac Kook, one of the 20th century's most important Orthodox rabbis and chief rabbi of Palestine. Rav[2] Kook saw no need to disprove evolution. Indeed, he saw Darwin's theory as pointing to "the unfolding of the spiritual dimension of existence, which does not show a hiatus of a single wasted step."

Evolution, said Rav Kook, might cause a sense of conflict within the religious views of the masses but it couldn't disturb the inner truth of Judaism.

"For this," he wrote, "there is need of great illumination, which is to penetrate all strata of society, until it reaches with its agreeable harmonization even the simplest circles of the masses."[3]

Rav Kook's faith-filled response to science contrasts with that of Klinghoffer and his colleagues in the Intelligent Design movement, desperately looking for God at the final line of the scientific enterprise.

---

[1]   Klinghoffer enjoys insulting his ideological opponents. Throughout the book he takes particular pleasure in a convoluted bit of reasoning which enables him to brand liberals as guilty of "*tumah*-thinking," using the Hebrew word generally translated as "unclean," "impure," or "taboo," but, in the tenor of his rhetoric, might best be rendered "cooties."

[2]   "Rav" is Hebrew for rabbi. Out of respect for Rabbi Kook, I'm departing from my usual style of omitting honorifics after the first reference.

[3]   Orot Hakodesh II 556-560. Translated in Bokser, Ben Zion, *The Essential Writings of Abraham Isaac Kook*, p.172, reprint edition Teaneck, NJ: Ben Yehuda Press, 2006.

They insist that science proves the scientific impossibility of evolution. This insistence proves ever more challenging, in part because our understanding of biochemistry and molecular genetics deepens with every passing year. Whether Klinghoffer likes it or not, we are currently graced with a deeper understanding of how the world works.

That is why Intelligent Design is rightly ridiculed for worshiping a "God of the gaps," a deity whose existence is found in those joints in which science fails to adequately explain every natural phenomenon. The majesty of a God cast in this image decreases with every new scientific study.

From a pragmatic standpoint, it's not good to bet against science being able to describe the universe. Certainly the Catholic Church did itself no favors when it placed its theological bets against the astronomical discoveries of Copernicus and Galileo.

The Church, like Klinghoffer, would have done well to follow the path of Maimonides, who when he argued against Aristotle's theory of the eternity of the world, did so only because "the theory has not been proved" (Guide II 25). Maimonides allowed that if the theory were scientifically proven, it would still not contradict the core Jewish beliefs.[4]

(Maimonides' willingness to interpret the Torah figuratively places him at odds with today's ultra-Orthodox Creationists, who insist the world is less than 6,000 years old and ban dinosaurs from their classrooms.)

The true beauty of Rav Kook's approach, however, is not its pragmatism but its piety. He believes that God is the premise, not the conclusion. His God is not ascertained in scientific arguments but through perception and faith.

In marked contrast to Klinghoffer's fear, Rav Kook reacts to those

---

[4]   Klinghoffer responds by quoting Maimonides on the doctrine of creation but, typically, leaves out the relevant point: Maimonides' disclaimer that he supported the doctrine of creation (that the world was not, as Aristotle had maintained, eternal) because of logical, philosophical reason, rather than Biblical proofs. Maimonides said that had Aristotle been proven correct, he would have reinterpreted the Bible accordingly. In other words, no matter how apparently important a theological doctrine, Maimonides would follow reason rather than revelation.

who postulate a purely physical world with equanimity, regarding "this childish construction as one which fashions the outer shell of life while not knowing how to build life itself."[5]

Rav Kook explicitly rejects the very moral logic of seeking God through the scientific means: "We do not base our faith in God on an inference from the existence of the world, or the character of the world, but on inner sensibility, on our disposition for the divine (ibid.)."

Rav Kook's perspective, for all its poetry, is a "no-brainer" for any Jew who takes his prayerbook seriously.

In the morning, when we praise God for "mercifully shining light on the Earth and those who dwell on it," we are not claiming that physics is inadequate to explain the sunrise. Rather, we see the nuclear furnace 93 million miles away as a reflection of God.

The next line tells us a key fact for a believing Jew: "God constantly renews the work of creation." Our prayerbook does not deny the materialistic mechanism of the sunrise, whether it be a heavenly chariot or an enactment of the laws of gravity. It asserts only that the rising of the sun reflects God's will, constancy and love.

We believe that God maintains each spinning electron not because we can think of no better explanation for physics but because that is our core belief about God. And our belief in God does not preclude our working to examine and understand the workings of His world as fully as is possible. Indeed, seen this way, our explorations are an appreciation and celebration of God's wondrous hand.

For Rav Kook the developing conception of science is important because we must raise our conception of God higher and higher in order to keep up. Conversely, Rav Kook would argue that atheism among evolutionary theorists is not a sign that something is wrong with biological science, but rather as a sign that something is wrong with a religion which proves inadequate to the challenges of science.

Rav Kook would argue that Klinghoffer should put aside his battle with science and seek instead to penetrate the inner meaning of Torah's mystical core: "In general this is an important principle in the conflict

5   Igrot I 44, Bokser p. 199-200

of ideas, that when an idea comes to negate some teaching in the Torah, we must not, to begin with, reject it, but build the edifice of the Torah above it, and thereby we ascend higher, and through this ascent, the ideas are clarified."[6]

Fully imbued with the constant presence of God, Rav Kook might well ask with outrage: How can Klinghoffer reject the "atheist scientists'" materialistic explanation for the origins of life, but accept their materialistic explanation for the orbits of the planets? Why shouldn't Klinghoffer come out and demand a physics, a chemistry, and a geology that show the hand of God?

As believers, we accept that God chose to create a world governed by natural laws, even though a world that operated *without* them might provide clearer evidence of God's hand. Biology is not the only field in which God's presence may seem obscured.

Klinghoffer's problem is that at his core, his soul is that of a plodding materialist, not a mystic.

"There is simply no way to reconcile an idea with its precise negation," he argued against me, and against Rav Kook, in the *Jerusalem Post*.

Sure there is, replies the mystic. God, the confluence of opposites, reconciles all ideas. God is the unity behind the apparent multiplicity. (Those less theologically-minded can also refer to Hegelian synthesis). That Klinghofer discards Rav Kook's theology as easily as he discards scientific facts that don't fit his agenda is a sad reminder that Klinghoffer is ultimately a man of politics—*not* a man of faith.

Klinghoffer accuses me of not making a choice between God and materialism, of "dancing at two weddings" in the Yiddish parlance. That accusation might better be aimed at Klinghoffer's own enterprise of "intelligent design," which can't decide whether it's a faith-based enterprise or a (pseudo) scientific discipline.

Actually, it *has* been decided; in the case *Tammy Kitzmiller, et al. v. Dover Area School District, et al* in Pennsylvania in 2005, in which 11

6   Igrot I 134; Bokser p.79

parents sued the school board that mandated that "intelligent design" be presented in class as an alternative to evolution. The judge ruled for the plaintiffs, agreeing that "intelligent design" was nothing other than a repackaging of creationism, the religious belief that the creation story in Genesis 1 trumps all evidence that the cosmos is billions of years old.

That's why Klinghoffer and his colleagues have to simultaneously pretend that there is a scientific dispute that "may be debated by reasonable and intelligent people," even while raising the theological stakes: "Darwinism would put God out of business."

Klinghoffer is correct when he says, "Darwin undercuts such belief [in God] in favor of atheism." But that makes it a challenge to religion; it doesn't make it *false*.

Unfortunately for Klinghoffer's God, there really is no scientific debate, other than that fueled by Klinghoffer's own Discovery Institute for its own religious purposes.

And those religious purposes are *not* Jewish purposes.

The Center for Science and Culture, a project of the Discovery Institute, declared its "wedge" strategy in 1999: "Design theory promises to reverse the stifling dominance of the materialistic worldview, and to *replace it with a science consonant with Christian and theistic convictions.*" Also: "If we view the predominant materialistic science as a giant tree, our strategy is intended to function as a wedge that, while relatively small, can split the trunk when applied at its weakest points."

And what of the objectives of the funders of the Institute? Let us take stock of the members of Team Discovery.

There is the Tennessee-based Maclellan Foundation, which describes itself as "committed to the infallibility of Scripture, to Jesus Christ as Lord and Savior, and to the fulfillment of the Great Commission." Jewish? Not so much.

And then there's the Lynde and Harry Bradley Foundation, which prior to supporting the Discovery Institute, supported the far-right John Birch Society.[7] Not really anyone the Goldbergs want to play ca-

---

[7]   The John Birch Society trafficked in anti-Semitic stereotypes, but expelled

nasta with.

Fieldstead & Co., owned by Howard and Robert Ahmanson, has donated heavily to the Institute. Ahmanson served for over two decades at a Christian Dominionist think tank, where he was a major donor as well. "Dominionism" is the idea that Christians should wrest "dominion" over America. One of the prime goals of the movement is to eradicate religious freedom and convert the world to Christianity. Not too cozy for the other religions when you consider that Dominionists believe that people who do not worship the way they do court the death penalty. Sounds like the pogroms my wife's grandmother used to reminisce about, and not too fondly, either.

It gets harder to ignore when you take a look at Dominionist literature from the pen of one of their earlier major writers, David Chilton:

> The god of Judaism is the devil. The Jew will not be recognized by God as one of His chosen people until he abandons his demonic religion and returns to the faith of his fathers—the faith which embraces Jesus Christ and His Gospel.[8]

So how does an "Orthodox Jew" like Klinghoffer suffer these people? How does he cash in those paychecks? And why does he champion Intelligent Design? Jews have plenty of issues, but Intelligent Design is not one of them: As the Orthodox Rabbinical Council of America put it in 2005, "significant Jewish authorities have maintained that evolu-

---

members for *overt* anti-Semitism. "In a sense," wrote Chip Berlet and Matthew Lyons in their book *Right Wing Populism in America: Too Close for Comfort*, "the Birch society pioneered the encoding of implicit cultural forms of ethnocentric White racism and Christian nationalist antisemitism rather than relying on the White supremacist biological determinism and open loathing of Jews that had typified the old right prior to WWII."

[8]   David Chilton, "The Days of Vengeance: An Exposition of the Book of Revelation", Dominion Press, Ft. Worth, TX (1984), p.127. Later, Chilton was decried as a heretic, but this book is still published, distributed and publicly approved by Dominion Press.

tionary theory, properly understood, is not incompatible with belief in a Divine Creator, nor with the first 2 chapters of Genesis."

And those Orthodox rabbis who reject evolution have no problem rejecting physics too and insisting the world is less than 6,000 years old. (One survey of Orthodox students at a New York area public university found that 28 percent believed scientists were lying about evolution—and that 73 percent believed the world was thousands of years old, not billions. Further, 12 percent believed the sun revolved around the earth. The parents of *those* kids might well wish to have their yeshiva tuition refunded.)

Most Orthodox rabbis—whether they believe in a young or ancient universe—would be inclined to turn Klinghoffer's query back upon him, and question why he insists upon dancing between two opinions? Why insist the world is ancient, as described by science, but not accept evolution? Why insist on the priority of theology, but not take the Torah's description of creation seriously?

The answer lies in Christian sociology, in the needs of American Christians. Where strict Orthodox Jews grudgingly understand the need to educate their children privately because they want their children trained in a non-mainstream fashion, fundamentalist Christians take any defection of their imperial claims personally. Sensitivity to others is not a hallmark of conservative Christians.[9]

As a Jew, I don't expect the broader culture to support my faith; I'm grateful for the occasions when they tolerate it. So if science doesn't

---

[9]   Take for example the question of the calendar, where the question of using "b.c.e." instead of "b.c." can arouse heated emotions. At its year 2000 convention at Orlando FL, the Southern Baptist Convention approved their Resolution 9: "On retaining the traditional method of calendar dating (B.C./A.D.)." With reference to the popularity of the CE/BCE nomenclature, it stated, in part: "...This practice is the result of the secularization, anti-supernaturalism, religious pluralism, and political correctness pervasive in our society." Further, "The traditional method of dating is a reminder of the preeminence of Christ and His gospel in world history." The resolution recommended that Southern Baptist "individuals, churches, entities, and institutions... retain the traditional method of dating and avoid this revisionism."

The website religioustolerance.org reports having gotten virulent hate mail from Christians outraged over its neutral discussion of this controversy.

firm up my children's faith, that's okay; that's not its job. Klinghoffer would rather misrepresent science to get a conclusion more in keeping with his theological well being. Frankly, my theological problems would be reduced if the Holocaust hadn't happened—but that's no reason to become a Holocaust denier.

But Klinghoffer has become a Holocaust denier after a fashion, promoting the notion that a straight line can be drawn between Charles Darwin and Adolph Hitler.[10] Here's what the Anti-Defamation League had to say about an anti-evolution film that Klinghoffer promoted:

> The film "Expelled: No Intelligence Allowed" misappropriates the Holocaust and its imagery as a part of its political effort to discredit the scientific community which rejects so-called intelligent design theory.
>
> Hitler did not need Darwin to devise his heinous plan to exterminate the Jewish people and Darwin and evolutionary theory cannot explain Hitler's genocidal madness.
>
> Using the Holocaust in order to tarnish those who promote the theory of evolution is outrageous and trivializes the complex factors that led to the mass extermination of European Jewry.

Such beliefs have been accurately described as a form of Holocaust denial because blaming Darwin frees the Nazis and everyone else from responsibility. It's a particularly useful tactic for those who don't want to confront the result of racial supremacy and hate.

Is this really how God would run a school board?

Klinghoffer returns to his metaphor of the battle between Elijah and the priests of Baal for the souls of Israel. He proposes that test, in which both sides built an altar, be reenacted. In the original version, Elijah

---

10   See, for example, "Think About The Connection Between Hitler And Darwin," published 4/18/2008 at http://www.jewcy.com/post/there_connection_between_hitler_and_darwin

built an altar, and the priests of Baal built an altar, but fire descended only upon Elijah's altar.

In Klinghoffer's contemporary version, instead of altars, there are lecterns in a high school auditorium. Instead of sacrifices, there are arguments. And instead of heavenly fire picking the winner, the students in a high school biology class would judge[11].

Seems like a pretty lame excuse for a remake, if you ask me.

In truth, we have no access to the altar or the fire of the prophet. But if the divine fire is lit in the souls of the faithful, then Baal holds no sway. Science becomes no threat to men of faith, but good clean fuel to make that soul fire burn even brighter and more true, adding to the heat of belief, the light required for clear vision.

---

[11]   See *How Would God Vote?* p.78

8

Taxation and Misrepresentation

How would you like to save on taxes? What would you say if I told you I knew a foolproof way to cut your tax bill by two-thirds and was willing to let you in on a secret? Would you be grateful?

Here's the secret: Simply don't report two-thirds of your income!

Now how do you feel? Hoodwinked? Disappointed? Angry that my suggestion is immoral, illegal, impractical and ineffective?

That bait-and-switch is the tack taken by David Klinghoffer when discussing taxation, as he twists a few Biblical passages to argue for lowering taxes on millionaires. Too bad that to answer the question of how would God *really* vote, you don't get to pick and choose your Biblical citations any more than you can choose which income to report to the Internal Revenue Service.

Klinghoffer argues that certain Biblical verses indicate God wants a specific Biblical tax rate. What he doesn't declare, however, are several Biblical passages indicating that God has a very different attitude toward the accumulation of wealth than do such "flat-tax" advocates as Steve Forbes. He also is going to show a great concern for the "tax rate," as if cutting taxes doesn't involve either raising debt or cutting government.

Sure, he'll make you feel good about voting for the candidate who promises to cut your taxes—but his argument is as shady as a bogus tax shelter.

Let's start with Klinghoffer's bottom line:

> God would vote for freedom, which would necessarily entail reducing the overall tax burden to reasonable levels, certainly below 20 percent.[1]

With that end in mind, Klinghoffer reads through a couple of Biblical passages.

With his first text, Klinghoffer shows how clearly he doesn't understand the notion of a social contract, of what differentiates a constitutional democracy "of the people, by the people, and for the people" from a Pharaonic dictatorship.

He cites a passage from Genesis 47. The seven years of famine predicted by Joseph are underway and Joseph, as Pharaoh's deputy, sells surplus grain back to the Egyptian people. This is how Klinghoffer tells it:

> When the famine hit, there was sufficient food to save the country from starvation. However, Joseph made the Egyptians sell themselves and their land to the king. "Joseph said to the people, 'Look—I have acquired you this day with your land for Pharaoh; here is seed for you—sow the land. At the ingathering of the harvests you will give a fifth to Pharaoh; the [other]

---

[1] Klinghoffer, p.105.

four parts shall be yours—as seed for the field, and
food for yourselves.'" In this way, the Egyptians agreed,
"We will be serfs to Pharaoh" (Genesis 47:23-25).[2]

Insists Klinghoffer: "Notice the equation of a 20 percent tax with
serfdom."

In other words, you only think you're free. The Bible—in Klinghoffer's ideological reading—is telling you you're a slave.

But Klinghoffer gets this all wrong. The Bible is not telling us to
see the 20 percent tax as slavery; rather, we're supposed to see the 20
percent tax on Pharaoh's serf as evidence of Joseph's righteousness. We
know this because the 20 percent tax was imposed originally not during
the seven years of famine, but during the seven years of harvest. Joseph
advised Pharaoh:

> Let Pharaoh do this, and let him appoint officers
> over the land, and take up the fifth part of the land
> of Egypt in the seven years of plenty. And let them
> gather all the food of those good years that come, and
> lay up grain under the hand of Pharaoh, and let them
> keep food in the cities. And that food shall be for store
> to the land against the seven years of famine, which
> shall be in the land of Egypt; that the land perish not
> through the famine. (Genesis 41:34-36)

Placing a 20 percent tax on the harvest during times of plenty arous-
es no controversy from the ruler, the people, nor the Bible. This is not
considered slavery. What turns the Egyptian people into serfs is the
imposition of market rate pricing on the stores of grain when the people
need them. First the people give all their money to Pharaoh. Then all
their cattle. Next, they give all their land—which gives Pharaoh an opportunity to resettle them, "And as for the people, he moved them to
cities from one end of the borders of Egypt to the other end of it." (Gen

---

[2] Klinghoffer, p.96.

47:21). Finally, having acquired ownership over all money, cattle, and land, Joseph acquires the people who accept the position of serfs, but are taxed like citizens. (We see what actual slavery looks like only a few chapters further on, in Exodus. Needless to say, it involves forced labor from dawn to dusk, not payroll deductions.)

Had Joseph implemented a liberal welfare economy, predicated on progressive taxation, the story would have been different. When the people were wealthy with surplus grain, he would have imposed the same 20 percent tax that successfully warded off the famine. But rather than demanding people forfeit all their property in exchange for food, and humbling them into destitute serfs, he would have provided the food as an entitlement to the population. After all, they had paid into the food security system from which the food stores were drawn! In this hypothetical scenario, Pharaoh would not have had all the money, would not have been able to relocate people across his kingdom on whim, and the Egyptian population would still be free.

On the other hand, had no taxes at all been imposed, the people would have kept their freedom—and starved to death. God's vote, judging from the dream he provided to Pharaoh and Joseph's interpretation, seems to have been for a liberal welfare state.

That Klinghoffer can't distinguish between a Communist regime owning all property and a liberal welfare state financed through an income tax shows how intense are his ideological blinders, as does his failure to notice that God emphatically did not vote for a libertarian tax-free market-driven solution to the problems of the Nile business cycle.

Another passage Klinghoffer brings is from the Book of Samuel. Samuel has been ruling Israel as a prophet. But he's getting old, and the people have decided that it's time for a king like other nations have.

Samuel is opposed to this new order, and he warns the people about the king: "He will take a tenth of your grain and vines... He will take a tenth of your sheep, and you will be his slaves." [I Samuel 8:15,17]

Struts Klinghoffer:

That's right, a 10 percent tax amounts to slavery.

Are we not slaves?[3]

And wouldn't you know it, Klinghoffer reminds us, we pay far more than 10% taxes!

This seems like a watertight Biblical case against taxes... unless you start thinking about it.

For one thing, this passage is clearly descriptive, not prescriptive. It sets out what a king might do—and is allowed to do. There is a similar passage about a king in Deuteronomy which is worth referring to.

> When you come to the land which the Lord your God gives you, and shall possess it, and shall live in it, and shall say, I will set a king over me, like all the nations that are around me; You shall set him king over you, whom the Lord your God shall choose; one from among your brothers shall you set king over you; you may not set a stranger over you, who is not your brother. But he shall not multiply horses to himself, nor cause the people to return to Egypt, to the end that he should multiply horses; for as much as the Lord has said to you, You shall henceforth return no more that way. Neither shall he multiply wives to himself, that his heart turn not away; nor shall he greatly multiply to himself silver and gold. [Deuteronomy 17:14-17]

Here the Torah is saying that a king will want to do certain things— and that they're not kosher. They're strictly forbidden. Notice, though, that the king is *not* barred from taxing the people. The Torah's restrictions lie not in the king's abilities to tax people, but about his purpose in collecting money and power. Does he want to return the people to Egypt? To multiply horses? To multiply wives? To multiply for himself silver and gold? The king will want to use his power of taxation selfishly, for his own aggrandizement, says Deuteronomy. But he is not

---

[3] Klinghoffer, p.97.

permitted.

Samuel's warning, and Deuteronomy's prohibitions, are better read as a call against self-serving spending (which could well include building up an army for aggressive wars of conquest designed to benefit the royal treasury rather than the populace), not a call against taxing.[4]

Which leads to the question: What are taxes for?

According to the Center on Budget and Policy Priorities, in 2007 22% of the federal budget went to defense; 21% to Social Security; another 21% to Medicare, Medicaid and the State Children's Health Insurance Program (SCHIP); 9% on safety net programs, 9% interest on the debt, and 18% everything else.

(As we'll see in the next chapter, Klinghoffer's policy prescriptions actually could have a major impact on federal tax rates, as his opposition to spending money on health care would let him eliminate the the fifth of the federal budget that goes to Medicare and other health programs, no doubt quickly reducing Social Security costs as well.)

On the whole, these expenditures aren't to enrich the government; they're to enable the government to execute its constituted task: "insure domestic tranquility, provide for the common defense, promote the general welfare, and secure the blessings of liberty to ourselves and our posterity."

Seems like God might not be so upset about this.

The problem with looking to lower the tax rates, as Klinghoffer wants us to do, is that decreasing tax rates decreases tax revenues, which increases budget deficits, which increases borrowing, which increases interest payments—but the Torah is very explicitly opposed to charging, or paying, interests on loans.[5]

---

4   For a thoughtful discussion of Samuel's complaints, albeit one focusing more on political than economic issues, see Silber, David, "Anarchy and Monarchy: Samuel the Prophet King" in Helfgot, Nathaniel, ed., *The Yeshivat Chovevei Torah Rabbinical School Tanakh Companion to the Book of Samuel*, Teaneck, NJ: Ben Yehuda Press, 2006.

5   Exodus 22:24: If you lend money to any of My people, even to the poor with thee, you shall not be to him as a creditor; neither shall you lay upon him interest.

(Practically speaking, the Torah would allow governments to pay interest, particularly to foreign creditors, such as the Chinese government which financed the Bush tax cuts. But remember, for Klinghoffer it's the principle that matters....) Given a choice between decreasing tax rates or decreasing deficits and interest payments, how would God *really* vote?

Klinghoffer sounds as if he is using religion to derive tax policy. But pay close attention, and you'll see rather that he is making a religion of the flat tax.

He is following in a tradition—stretching back to Ronald Reagan's earliest political speeches, in the 1950s—of using the Bible to discredit progressive taxation.

As Reagan explained the Biblical laws of tithes, "If the Lord prospers you 10 times as much, you are to give 10 times as much."[6] By golly, the Bible only had one tax bracket for the rich and the poor, so progressive taxation must be a Communist plot! If rich people pay a 35 percent tax rate (or as much as 70 percent during the Eisenhower administration when Reagan launched his campaign), and poor people pay 10 percent or even less—why, that's just not part of God's plan![7]

Let's take a moment to note what freedom Reagan was fighting for in the '50s: The freedom to pay a lower tax rate.[8]

Note which freedoms he wasn't fighting for. The freedom to vote. The freedom to be an equal citizen. While some people were marching,

---

[6]   Kiewe, Amos and Houck, Davis W., *A Shining City on a Hill: Ronald Reagan's Economic Rhetoric, 1951-1989*, Greenwood Publishing Group, 1991, p.17.

[7]   In 2002, the *Wall Street Journal* termed such people "lucky duckies." Neither the *Journal* nor Reagan spent much time worrying about the payroll taxes which fund Social Security and are regressive (that is, anti-progressive), taking a far higher share of a minimum wage worker's income than of, say, a corporate chief executive officer such as Halliburton's Dick Cheney.

[8]   I'm not necessarily arguing that the marginal tax rates of the post-war era were pragmatically optimal, though it's interesting that the American economy did roughly twice as well when the marginal tax rates were roughly twice as high. Here I'm focused on Reagan's and Klinghoffer's ideological points.

fighting and dying for the Biblical principle that all men are brothers, Ronald Reagan traveled the country fighting for the right of Hollywood actors to pay less taxes.

But that's OK, because half a century later, the leading conservative anti-tax activist would say that fighting against taxes wasn't just fighting for civil rights—it was fighting against the Holocaust.

In an October, 2003 interview with Terry Gross, Grover Norquist, the head of Americans for Tax Reform and the reputed architect of President Bush's tax cuts compared the morality of taxing the rich at higher rates to the Holocaust. Here's what he said:

> NORQUIST: The argument that some who play to the politics of hate and envy and class division will say is, "Well, that's only 2 percent — or, as people get richer, 5 percent, in the near future — of Americans likely to have to pay [the estate tax]." I mean, that's the morality of the Holocaust: "Oh, it's only a small percentage. It's not you; it's somebody else." And [in] this country, people who may not make earning a lot of money the centerpiece of their lives — they may have other things to focus on — they just say it's not just. If you've paid taxes on your income, government should leave you alone, not tax you again.
>
> GROSS: Excuse me one second. Did you just compare the estate tax with the Holocaust?
>
> NORQUIST: No, the morality that says it's okay to do something to a group because they're a small percentage of the population is the morality that says that the Holocaust is okay because they didn't target everybody. "It's just a small percentage, what are you worried about? It's not you. It's not you. It's them." And arguing that it's okay to loot some group because it's them, or kill some group because it's them — and because it's a small number—has no place in a democratic

society that treats people equally. The government's going to do something to or for us; it should treat us all equally. And the argument that Bill Clinton used when he wanted to raise taxes in 1993 is "I'm only going to tax the top 2 percent, so this doesn't affect the rest of you. I'm only going to get some of these guys, not you, others."

The challenge there, when people use that rhetoric —in addition to the fact that I think it's immoral to separate the society—but when South Africa divided society by race, that was wrong. When East Germany divided them by income and class, that was wrong. East Germany was not an improvement over South Africa. Dividing people so when you can mug them one at a time is a bad thing to do. Whether you do on racial grounds, religious grounds, whether-you-work-on-Saturdays-or-not grounds, economic grounds.

GROSS: So you see taxes as being, the way they are now, a terrible discrimination against the wealthy, comparable to the kind of discrimination of, say, the Holocaust?

NORQUIST: Well, when you pick, when you use different rhetoric, or different points for different purposes, and I would argue that those who say "Don't let this bother you, I'm only doing it — the government is only doing it — to a small part of the population," that is very wrong. And it's immoral. They should treat everybody the same. They shouldn't be shooting anyone. And they shouldn't be taking half of anybody's income or wealth when they die.

As *Washington Post* columnist Richard Cohen observed,

In fact, the moral equivalency Norquist concocts

[between the estate tax and the Holocaust] is his own
—and it speaks volumes about the 'morality' of anti-
tax Republicans. To them, the rich owe nothing— just
like the poor, they would say. (The difference between
rich and poor escapes them.) This is unbridled selfish-
ness in the guise of ideology and makes wealth the
moral equivalent of ethnicity or religion or even sexual
preference. To Norquist, distinguishing between rich
and poor is like making a selection at Auschwitz. It
not only trivializes the Holocaust, it collapses all moral
distinctions.

Now, you wouldn't know from listening to David Klinghoffer and
Ronald Reagan and Grover Norquist[9], but most religious Americans
have had no problem with taxing rich people at a higher rate than poor
people.

Klinghoffer does have a point: that's not how taxes work in the Torah.

Biblical tithes are a straight 10 percent. And there's a temple poll
tax of one-half shekel—a clearly regressive tax, that hurts the poor for
whom a half shekel might be a significant sum.

But as one scholar has noted[10], the realities of even a simple tithe in
an agricultural economy that hadn't yet discovered the zero were ex-
ceedingly complex. The rabbis in the Mishna delineate the various ways
farmers can choose to tithe: by quantity, by volume, by number. It was

---

[9]   Norquist's bizarre blend of accounting principles and Holocaust theology
was far from the first time the moral sense of this premiere Republican organizer ven-
tured in unusual directions. In 1985 he worked with Jack Abramoff to promote Ango-
lan guerrilla leader Jonas Savimbi with the assistance of the South African Apartheid
government. (See Frank, Thomas, *The Wrecking Crew: How Conservatives Rule*, Met-
ropolitan Books 2008, p.65)

[10]   Chodorow, Adam, "Biblical Tax Systems and the Case for Progressive Taxation" . Journal of Law and Religion, Vol. 23, No. 1, 2007 Available at SSRN: http://
ssrn.com/abstract=1013655

not a simple question, particularly since the tithe had to be taken before the food could be eaten. (As opposed to American taxes, which don't have to be precisely calculated until the tax year is concluded.)

> "Given these difficulties, the decision to use a flat ten percent rate to determine the tithe likely reflects the need to make the tithe workable under the conditions of ancient agriculture and was not a conscious decision that proportionate taxation reflects a divine sentiment regarding distributive justice."

What makes Klinghoffer's attempt to hold a Biblical discussion of taxes so bizarre is his failure to grapple with—or even acknowledge—the most basic institutions of Biblical economics. Note that these are not obscure verses, apparent throw-away lines raised up to be given great interpretive import. No, these are lengthy passages with clear statements about what Conservatives term "economic freedom."

> "And you shall hallow the fiftieth year, and proclaim liberty throughout all the land to all the inhabitants of it; it shall be a jubilee to you; and you shall return every man to his possession, and you shall return every man to his family.... In the year of this jubilee you shall return every man to his possession. And if you sell something to your neighbor, or buy something from your neighbor's hand, you shall not defraud one another; According to the number of years after the jubilee you shall buy from your neighbor, and according to the number of years of the fruits he shall sell to you; According to the multitude of years you shall increase its price, and if the years are few, you shall accordingly diminish its price; for according to the number of the years of the fruits does he sell to you. You shall not therefore defraud one another; but you shall fear your God; for I am the Lord your God. Therefore you shall do my statutes, and keep my judgments, and do them; and you shall dwell in the land in safety. [Lev. 25:10-18]

Every 50 years is the Jubilee, and all real estate returns to the descendants of its original owner. All slaves go free. Is this raw capitalism? Is this the free hand of an unregulated market?

No. This is the Torah saying: There is a limit. Money and wealth can go so far—but it's not an inalienable right. Having grown richer than your neighbor today doesn't mean you can keep his field forever. In an agricultural society, where owning land was the key to creating wealth, this was a severe limit one's "freedom" to grow rich and turn one's neighbors into serfs.

Talk about a redistribution of wealth!

Klinghoffer's failure to discuss this passage—which underlies much Jewish and Christian economic thinking in recent centuries—is telling. It's not that the law of the Jubilee is obscure; Klinghoffer hears it read in the synagogue every year. And it's not that the law of the Jubilee is no longer practiced, for a multitude of reasons—because Klinghoffer's avowed aim is to look for political lessons from the Bible, not to directly enact Mosaic law.

No, Klinghoffer omits the Jubilee because its message undercuts a central tenet of American conservative politics for at least half a century. Because with the institution of the Jubilee (and the related institution of the Sabbatical year, which bans agricultural work every seventh year), the Torah shows that the argument posed by conservatives against Roosevelt's New Deal—that it is indistinguishable from Communist tyranny—is false. The Bible indeed paints a middle, third way between full state control of the economy and the complete laissez-faire approach favored by conservatives.

In looking for the Bible to support laissez-faire economics, ideologues like Klinghoffer must simultaneously pretend there are only two economic possibilities (the fallacy of the false dichotomy) and rip out pages from the Bible.

Besides the Leviticus passages about the Jubilee, Klinghoffer's Bible readings neglected whole books, such as that of the prophet Amos,[11]

---

[11]   Klinghoffer's twin omissions are also committed by Rabbi Yosef Yitzhak

who famously warned that the fate of Israel hinged on how the rich treated the poor:

> And I will smite the winter-house with the summer-house; and the houses of ivory shall perish, and the great houses shall have an end, says the LORD. [Amos 3:15]
>
> Therefore, because you trample upon the poor, and take from him exactions of wheat; you have built houses of hewn stone, but you shall not dwell in them, ye have planted pleasant vineyards, but you shall not drink wine thereof.
>
> For I know how manifold are your transgressions, and how mighty are your sins; you that afflict the just, that take a ransom, and that turn aside the needy in the gate. [5:11-12]
>
> Hear this, O you that would swallow the needy, and destroy the poor of the land, Saying: 'When will the new moon be gone, that we may sell grain? and the sabbath, that we may set forth corn? making the ephah small, and the shekel great, and falsifying the balances of deceit; That we may buy the poor for silver, and the needy for a pair of shoes, and sell the refuse of the corn?' [8:4-6]

These are not the preachings of a free-market prophet. As Reverend Jim Wallis says:

> The Hebrew prophet's condemnation of the cor-

Lifshitz. a Senior Fellow in the Institute for Philosophy, Politics and Religion of the Shalem Center, the Israeli conservative think tank supported in large measure by Republican billionaire Sheldon Adelson. In a 33-page essay that Klinghoffer praises as "brilliant," and which claims to provide "Foundations of a Jewish Economic Theory" Lifshitz fails to mention either the institution of the Jubilee or the concerns of Amos and his fellow prophets for the poor.

rupt wealth of his era applies quite dramatically to our current situation. Amos lived in a time not unlike our own—one of great prosperity, but prosperity built upon corruption and oppression, leading to a great and growing inequality.[12]

Given these concerns of the prophets, those who fear God might do well to wonder at the ways that President Bush used tax cuts to wage economic warfare against 90 percent of the American people. At a time when much the "conservative" movement has become a mechanism of class warfare by the extremely wealthy against the rest of America, this selective read of scriptures is a useful weapon.[13]

This shift of wealth is in part the direct result of the un-Biblical approach taken by the Bush tax cuts, which Senator McCain now wants to extend. In particular, and a central target of Bush and conservatives, was the Estate Tax, which is scheduled to be eliminated altogether in 2010.

The premise of the estate tax, originally instituted in 1916, was the same as that of the Jubilee laws: It is against the interest of society (and

---

[12]   Wallis, Jim, *God's Politics: Why the Right Gets It Wrong and the Left Doesn't Get It,* HarperSanFrancisco, 2005, p.266.

[13]   Some statistics from inequality.org, a website of Demos, a non-partisan public policy research and advocacy organization: All of the income gains in 2005 went to the top 10 percent of households, while the bottom 90 percent of households saw income declines. The top one percent of households received 21.8 percent of all pre-tax income in 2005, more than double what that figure was in the 1970s. (The top one percent's share of total income bottomed out at 8.9 percent in 1976.) This is the greatest concentration of income since 1928, when 23.9 percent of all income went to the richest one percent. The above figures include capital gains, which are strongly affected by the ups and downs of the financial markets. Excluding capital gains, the richest one percent claimed 17.4 percent of all pre-tax income in 2005, more than double what that figure was in the 1970s. (It bottomed out at 7.8 percent in 1973.) This is the greatest concentration of income since 1936, when the richest one percent received 17.6 percent of total income. Between 1979 and 2005, the top five percent of American families saw their real incomes increase 81 percent. Over the same period, the lowest-income fifth saw their real incomes decline 1 percent. In 1979, the average income of the top 5 percent of families was 11.4 times as large as the average income of the bottom 20 percent. In 2005, the ratio was 20.9 times.

according to the Bible, the will of God) for fortunes to ever accumulate. Money makes money; the wealthy find it easier to make more wealth, by fair means or foul.

Teddy Roosevelt explicitly took this view when he endorsed the estate tax in 1906, saying that its "primary objective should be to put a constantly increasing burden on the inheritance of those swollen fortunes, which it is certainly of no benefit to this country to perpetuate[14]."

All things considered, it seems unlikely that God would *really* vote to repeal the estate tax.

The war against progressive taxation waged by Reagan, Bush and Klinghoffer is nothing new. Rabbi Yom Tov Lipmann Heller was an early victim in the war... back in the 17th century. My teacher Rabbi Joseph B. Soloveitchik relayed the story as an example of how "the greatest rabbis throughout the millennia displayed their greatness in the sphere of social justice."[15]

Rav Soloveitchik related that Rabbi Heller "was assigned the responsibility of deciding on the distribution of liability for taxes within the Jewish community and for turning over the money to the civil authorities. He instituted a system of progressive taxation so that the wealthy paid more and the poor less. For this supposed inequity he was jailed and was in danger of losing his life."

This was a true example of class warfare, the wealthy class against the rest. It is the warfare that Amos spoke out against, and which Klinghoffer and his tax polemics exemplify.

However tempting it may be to take shelter within Klinghoffer's comforting rhetoric as you complain about your taxes, the truth is that you're being conned. Taxation is not slavery, progressive taxation is not a Holocaust, and God would not really vote to repeal the estate tax.

---

[14]   Cited in *Death by a Thousand Cuts: The Fight Over Taxing Inherited Wealth* by Michael J. Graetz, Ian Shapiro 2005 Princeton University Press

[15]   *The Rav: The World of Rabbi Joseph B. Soloveitchik* by Aaron Rakeffet-Rothkoff, Joseph Epstein, KTAV, 1999, vol 2 p. 48

9

Health Care: Conservatives Will Make You Sick

Rabbi Israel Salanter, the great 19th century Jewish moralist, used to describe the difference between a *Tzadik*, a righteous man, and a *Rasha*, a wicked man, as follows: A *Tzadik* worries about his own soul and his neighbor's body. A *Rasha* is concerned about his own body and his neighbor's soul.

In that case, Klinghoffer, who seems to worry a good deal more about his fellow citizen's souls than about their bodies, is not a righteous man.

We've seen his concern for their souls—for their true "empowerment" as wives and mothers, for preserving the "purity" of their marriages.

This well being, as we've seen, is more important than their right to make their own choices. (Klinghoffer strikes a similar tone in his chapter on censorship, later in the book).

But when it comes to the bodies of his fellow Americans, he is much less concerned.

We'll see this when we discuss his "pro-choice" stance on smoking tobacco. And we see it most strongly in his chapter on health care.

To put it bluntly: Klinghoffer wants to protect your right to not have health insurance.

His conservative case against reform in health care policy is nothing like one of those debates during a Democratic primary, where complicated calculations and projections are tossed back and forth, and alternate economic forecasting models make competing claims, and decisions are weighed between different groups who stand to gain or lose based on the details of a policy change.

His case is much simpler.

He cherishes your right to be sick.

Now, if you're suffering a horrible disease, and are unable to treat it properly because you lack health insurance and adequate health care, you might not be overly impressed that Klinghoffer has not one but *two* reasons for supporting your present state.

I'll review them. But before I do, I want to review the Jewish law on the topic, as interpreted by one of the leading Orthodox authorities on Jewish medical law. This is one of the few cases where I will be presenting Torah commandments that actually *can* be fulfilled in the privacy of the voting booth.

According to Rabbi Moshe Tendler, who has trained generations of rabbis at Yeshiva University, there are three biblical commandments that obligate us with regard to healing.

☞   The first commandment is the verse used by the Talmud to justify the practice of medicine: "*urapo yirapeh*—to heal you shall heal." (Exodus 21: 19) Literally, this means, "he shall surely be healed," but the Talmud reads the double verb as a positive obligation to heal the sick. The doctor has the obligation to heal people, but people also have an obligation to go to the doctor. For those who say, "God will heal me," the Talmud is saying that you can't go to the "True Doctor" (God) unless you go to the earthly doctor first!

☞ The second commandment comes from Deuteronomy 22:2: "And if thy brother be not nigh unto thee, or if thou know him not, then thou shalt bring it unto thine own house, and it shall be with thee until thy brother seek after it, and thou shalt restore it to him again." (The Talmud reasons that if we have an obligation to restore a person's lost property, we certainly have an obligation to restore his lost health.)

☞ The third commandment comes from Leviticus (19:16): "*lo ta'amod al dam re'echa*" —do not stand on your brother's blood." It is not enough to "do no harm"; we are commanded to actively help.

Taken together, says Rabbi Tendler, these speak not only to an obligation upon a doctor to heal, but upon society as well. There is a collective responsibility to restore our brother's lost health, and to make certain that we do not stand idly by while he dies.

In other words: health care is a societal responsibility—certainly in Jewish discourse.

Before commencing analysis of a Talmudic discussion, one of my teachers at Yeshiva University used to say, "Put on your diving suit! We're going deep."

Alas, as we prepare to wade through Klinghoffer's muddy arguments concerning health care, we are clearly not swimming in the sea of Talmud.

Here's a paragraph of Klinghoffer:

> Mandating what seems to be common sense (making sure you have health coverage), and precluding the individual's freedom to take his chances if he prefers, places "universal health care" on the list of those other liberal political notions that foreclose free choice and moral responsibility. We saw earlier that John Edwards includes in his vision of universal coverage the requirement that Americans consult a doctor regularly. The

Bible emphatically insists that adults be given responsibility. Market solutions to problems like our health care "crisis," whatever their other virtues, cast citizens as responsible individual moral actors. For that reason alone, the Bible would be opposed to most liberal schemes to fix health care.[1]

Here are some things wrong with this paragraph.

First is the unstated assumption that people who don't have health insurance don't have it because they *choose* not to have it. He "proves" this point on the next page with an anecdote of a colleague at the *National Review* who opted to go without health insurance for a period of time.

That's fine and dandy as anecdotes go (not all of Klinghoffer's stories are so benign) but hardly to the point. Health care policy analysts understand that it may be rational for young healthy people to decide not to lay out money for health insurance on the basis that it benefits others more than it benefits them as payees. That is precisely why health care analysts see the need to ratify policies that require full participation. Society is defining that health care is something that the healthy are obligated to provide for the sick.

This means that even healthy *National Review* writers have to pay taxes for health care, or in lieu of that, buy mandatory health insurance.

But in attempting to generalize from his colleague, Klinghoffer moves from the rhetorical to the ridiculous. He turns this anecdote— the story of a healthy person deciding that in the short run it pays to go without health insurance—into the story of Job choosing to suffer, yet keep his wealth.[2]

The question is: Do the colleague's health insurance payments truly make the difference between his wealth and his poverty? It is clear from the context that the story is *not* making that point. This fellow clearly

---

[1] Klinghoffer, p.119.
[2] Klinghoffer, p.120.

has discretionary income beyond his health care fees.

The truth is that, it is far more common for poverty and poor health to *coincide,* whether the poverty leads to the failure to maintain good health and cure illness, or whether in fact the cost of health care itself depletes resources and impoverishes families.

In 2001, an estimated two million Americans experienced medical bankruptcy. Among those whose illnesses led to bankruptcy, more than three quarters had insurance at the onset of illness, but out-of-pocket costs averaged nearly $12,000 since the start of illness.[3] While Klinghoffer might suggest that these families should have kept their $12,000, it seems likely that avoiding treatment would easily have cost them that much in wages lost to illness and premature death.

Klinghoffer is also concerned lest someone's free will be tarnished by attending a doctor. Throughout, he seems surprisingly unconcerned, for someone purporting to be a religious Jew, with how he is to fulfill his obligation to heal the sick and not stand by his brother's blood.

Taking seriously the obligation to safeguard health on a broad, social level, it becomes clear that the best way for us to fulfill these commandments is through communal action.

In the Talmud, there is a discussion of the passage in the Bible when Jacob prepares himself to meet his brother Esau, at the Jabbok River.

> "And Jacob was left alone." (Genesis 32:25) Said R. Eleazar: He remained behind for the sake of some small jars. Hence [it is learnt] that to the righteous their money is dearer than their body; and why is this? Because they do not stretch out their hands to robbery. (Talmud Hullin 91a)

---

3   See "MarketWatch: Illness and Injury as Contributors to Bankruptcy" *Health Affairs: the Policy Journal of the Health Sphere,* by David U. Himmelstein, et al(February 2005). (http://content.healthaffairs.org/cgi/content/full/hlthaff. w5.63/DC1)

David Klinghoffer quotes his teacher Rabbi Daniel Lapin as arguing that this in effect says that greed is good: That you're better off not
spending all your money on health care, because better to be wealthy
and sick than poor and healthy. Klinghoffer writes:

> [I]f we had to make such a choice, the Bible would
> have us chose wealth over health. It would be a shame
> if government policies, namely the imposition of uni-
> versal health care, were implemented to make it im-
> possible for a consumer to exercise such a risky but
> idealistic choice.[4]

(Let it be clear that that this is an interpretation of the Talmud that
is wholly original. Traditional interpretations, unlike that of Rabbi
Lapin, do not conform to the anti-Semitic stereotype of the money-
grubbing Jew.[5])

Having argued that money is better accumulated than spent on
health, Klinghoffer proceeds to argue that sickness is… good for you!

Like Rabbi Salanter's wicked *Rasha*, Klinghoffer wants to save your
soul at the cost of your body.

Klinghoffer approvingly quotes Catholic theologian Edward
Norman who argued that Catholicism and "secular humanism" have
two different attitudes toward suffering.

Klinghoffer quotes Norman as saying that Christianity "was found-

---

[4] Klinghoffer, p.121.

[5]   Rabbi Samson Raphael Hirsch, who Klinghoffer is found of quoting in
other contexts, explains that the Talmudic passage teaches "that the righteous ones
see even in the smallest value of honestly acquired fortune, something holy, which
they may neither squander nor allow to be uselessly wasted, and for the rightful use of
which they will be called to account. A million has, for them, only the value of a pin,
if it is a question of spending it for God-pleasing purposes, and a pin has the value of
a million if it is a question of wasting it uselessly. The smallest possession that he has,
who does not take anything by force, but only calls his own what he has acquired by
his honest toil, is considered by him as a token of God's Providence and Goodness,
his very smallest possession, a produce of honest sweat and God's Blessing and hence
of invaluable worth."

ed in an act of expiatory pain, has regarded human suffering as not only inseparable from the nature of life on earth, as a matter of observable fact, but also as a necessary condition in spiritual formation."

Norman contrasts this with those who value "the palliation of whatever humans themselves regard as the cause of their suffering or deprivation." In short, health care questions become a bitter choice between Jesus and antibiotics. (Norman seems to have forgotten that Jesus is reported to have *healed the sick* as part of his ministry!)

As we learned from Rabbi Tendler, it's clear that relieving and curing physical suffering is an obligation—whether it is our own, or someone else's physical suffering.

If that makes Rabbi Tendler a secular humanist—well, like most Orthodox Jews, he'd probably prefer that to being labeled a Catholic in good standing. (As Klinghoffer is so fond of forgetting, secular humanists never burnt Jewish bodies to save their souls.)

Norman's logic extends past health insurance. Note what Klinghoffer says, mocking Barack Obama:

> If materialism is the premise, then by all means, let us deploy the government to rid ourselves our illnesses—of all illness, why not?[6]

Government research and development efforts to eliminate polio, would set Klinghoffer jeering, "That's not government's job." He no doubt laments all the wasted opportunity for spiritual growth thrown away by the development of the polio vaccine. You can bet Klinghoffer would vote to defund the National Institute of Health.

(Most Americans, I suspect, would consider governments that are more concerned with the good of their citizen's souls than with their "life, liberty, and pursuit of happiness," and that prefer faith healing to medicine, to be benighted relics of the dark ages.)

Klinghoffer's efforts to pervert the Torah into a Catholic mold fail to convince even himself. Klinghoffer does not claim that he, *person-*

---

[6] Klinghoffer, p.125.

ally, is forgoing health insurance with an aim of building up his 401K retirement plan (though he says that it is the moral choice). Nor does he confess to withholding medical attention from himself or from his children, even though suffering is, as he says, good for the soul.

Could it be that really he is just selfishly concerned only about his own health, and selfishly inured to the suffering of other people's children?

Klinghoffer confesses that he has not reached a high spiritual level:

> The Talmud explains that in an ideal world, we would never consult doctors at all. A person with an illness would seek out spiritual guidance, not unlike the model of Christian Science. That we are allowed to use medicine is a lenience, a concession taking into account that few of us are up to the exalted spiritual level it would require to effect healing through repentance.[7]

Securing medical insurance for himself while foregoing it for others is not a failure to reach an "exalted spiritual level." It is base hypocrisy.

Perhaps what motivates opposition to universal health care among Klinghoffer and other conservatives is not their faith that markets work better than government, or even concern about freedom of choice.

Perhaps it is greed and hypocrisy, pure and simple.

There's an important lesson for us in the story of Jacob that Klinghoffer quotes from the Talmud.

True, our father Jacob risked his life for his possessions.

But he didn't risk the lives of his servants.

He only risked his own.

That may well be what makes Jacob righteous. Klinghoffer, who would save *his* money at the expense of *other people's* health, can make no such claim.

---

[7] Klinghoffer, p.124.

10

Capital Punishment:
The Great Social Cleanser

Perhaps the most startling note in Klinghoffer's pro-Death Penalty chapter has to do with Yeshiva University's Cardozo Law School's Innocence Project. Klinghoffer acknowledges that between 1989 and 2000 the Innocence Project saved 28 death row inmates from wrongful executions. This effort, according to Klinghoffer, illustrates how "even traditional [Jewish] denominations have buckled" under the popular— and "liberal"—anti-Capital Punishment trend.

We'll proceed to examine the rest of his arguments in a moment, but meanwhile, please, meditate on the notion that Jews working hard to free inmates who were about to be killed for no good reason is presented by Klinghoffer as a kind of failure of nerve, a succumbing of a Jewish university to the pressures of public opinion.

For the record, I, too, support the death penalty. But in Klinghoffer's place I would have celebrated the Innocence Project and the great service it provides to society and to our national reputation as a people who love the law.

Before I continue, let me establish a few fundamental notes about the functioning of the Sanhedrin, the higher Jewish court which deals with *dinei nefashot*, capital offenses:

- ☞ It is composed of 23 judges.
- ☞ To acquit it requires a simple majority (12-11).
- ☞ To convict it requires a 2-vote majority, which, mathematically, actually means a 3-vote span (13-10).
- ☞ If all 23 judges find a defendant guilty he goes free.
- ☞ Following a conviction, the judges are paired, one of each opinion, to deliberate the case overnight. If a convicting judge changes his mind, his vote counts towards acquittal, but an acquitting judge may not change his vote.

Klinghoffer pays lip service to the Talmud's declaration that a Sanhedrin which killed once in seventy years is called "murderous," but his translation of *katlanit* to mean "destructive," is a mistake, perhaps intended to downplay the vehemence of the statement. He even cites Rabbi Akiva, the shining light of classical Jewish law, who suggested that, had he been a member of Sanhedrin, no one would have ever been executed. Those are familiar attitudes, but when we see the above five procedural rules we must conclude that the high court was *rigged* by the sages to avoid executions.

Moreover, there is little in common between the US courts' approach to capital crimes and the Sanhedrin's. Here are a few rules of testimony before the Sanhedrin in capital cases:

- ☞ Gamblers, ranchers who abuse the environment, and others who don't contribute to the well- being of society may not testify.

☞   The deaf may not testify.
☞   The mentally retarded may not testify.
☞   Women may not testify.

However, boys 13 years and older may testify.

There is only one common denominator among the first four categories of refused witnesses: It is also questionable whether any of them would count towards a prayer quorum (*minyan*).

We have to ask why would the court bar information coming from a mature woman with a respected life experience and excellent judgment, while welcoming the testimony of a pimple-faced bar mitzvah boy. Certainly, the court's bias cannot stem from the quality of the testimony. So what are the judges looking for?

To try and understand, we should look into a wondrous ceremony prescribed by the Torah, known as the "Beheaded Heifer" (paraphrased for easier reading):

> If a person is found slain, lying in the field, and it is not known who killed them; then the local elders and judges must measure the distance from the corpse to the nearby towns. In the city which is nearest the slain man, the elders will take a heifer – which has not been used for any labor – to the bank of a running river, which is not plowed or sown, and break the heifer's neck there, under the direction of the priests. Then all the elders of that city will wash their hands over the dead heifer and say: "Our hands have not shed this blood, neither have our eyes seen it. Please, God, forgive your people Israel, and Suffer not innocent blood to remain in the midst of Your people Israel." Then the spilled blood shall be forgiven them. [Deut. 21:1-8].

The elders and judges in this tableau are the local Sanhedrin. They respond to the discovery of an unsolved capital crime with a proclamation of their innocence, lest the unredeemed blood of the slain stranger come back to haunt their town.

Do we really suspect that the elders of the town had anything to do with the murder? According to American law, the answer is a resounding No. However, in Jewish law, the elders *are* responsible. Not because *they* spilled the blood—this ceremony is intended for occasions when there *are* no witnesses and no basis for an accusation – but because the blood was spilled on their watch. And they must wash their hands of this blood or they'll face dire consequences, namely the wrath of God. It's a religious ceremony *par excellence*.

The proceedings of the greater Sanhedrin of 23 judges which judges a capital case is likewise a religious ceremony, with the identical mission: Put away innocent blood from the community's midst.

The stain of innocent spilled blood upon the spiritual well-being of society is the main reason I support the death penalty. I believe we collectively bear responsibility for the human suffering among us, and most of all for the slain. The social contract is threatened every time a murder goes unpunished.

Likewise, our spiritual well being is in jeopardy with every wrongful execution. Moreover, one could argue that the effect upon society of an individual murder is marginal compared to a wrongful execution by the state, which receives consent for its actions from you and me.

This is the reason the Sanhedrin's procedures during capital caes are so obviously skewed in favor of the accused: We shudder at the thought of society adding the blood of an innocent defendant to that of the victim's. Why else make it nearly impossible to execute anyone?

This is why it's quite disturbing to read Klinghoffer's note that *the Bible is well aware that human courts are human, prone to error,* and in that context (p.127) present the laws of false witnesses as the Bible's fail-safe method of guarding against human error. They are anything but fail-safe. Let's examine some of the rules for of false witnesses:

☞   The newer set of "nullifying" witnesses who come before the court to challenge the original witnesses may not bring conflict-ing testimony regarding the essence of the crime—they are lim-ited to testimony on time and place, specifically: At the time the original witnesses say they were viewing the crime, we saw the witnesses elsewhere.

☞   A third set of nullifying witnesses could come and disqualify the second set, thus re-qualifying the original witnesses, and a fourth to nullify the third, *ad nauseum.*

In other words, the rules regarding false witnesses are anything but fail-safe, and the court has no means of comparing conflicting, spe-cific, crime-related testimonies, nor can it block the potentially endless march of contradictory witnesses.

Klinghoffer does describe the law's expectation that the witnesses not only be sound enough to be counted in a prayer service, but must be actively involved in attempting to prevent the crime they witness – with some opinions suggesting they must spell out the nature of the crime as well as its precise punishment.

He does not mention that the law also requires those same witnesses to serve as executioners. Their hand must be the first to be raised to kill the convicted murderer.

My conclusion from all of the above is that the purpose of the Jew-ish capital trial is to cleanse the entire community of the horror of the spilled, innocent blood, lest it cry out of the soil to be avenged by God—who clarifies this point in His statement to the first murderer, Cain—"The voice of thy brother's blood cries unto Me from the ground."

Even Klinghoffer realizes that he cannot attribute to the Sanhedrin the blood-thirst of former Attorney General Alberto Gonzales or for-mer Texas Governor George W. Bush. So he invents a clever bypass to the obstacles facing the prosecution in capital cases:

> The resolution is found in the unique biblical di-vision of judicial functions into religious and secular

branches. When it comes to punishing murder, the importance of the religious court, the Sanhedrin, seems mainly symbolic. But the Bible assigns the secular government, the king, a role too, that is deadly serious and not symbolic at all.

He proceeds to cite from Maimonides' legal code, the *Mishneh Torah*, which assigns to the Jewish king the role of maintaining the social order. Following a considerable list of constitutional limits on the king's power, the code allows him to execute in the face of diminished proof: witnesses who did not get a clear view of the crime; witnesses who did not give the proper warning; and even in cases with a single witness.

What Klinghoffer is doing here is similar to what happened to the US government over the last eight years. Under the cover of a momentary national crisis, the executive branch maneuvered to eliminate some founding principles of American democracy, including the guarantees of the Fourth Amendment against unreasonable search and seizure and the law of *habeas corpus*.

Maimonides indeed permits the Jewish king, in a time of duress, to loosen the rules of evidence in favor of maintaining public order—but Klinghoffer mistakenly considers this the biblical *ideal*, dismissing the Sanhedrin's function as largely symbolic.

Can it be that despite the Bible's lengthy paragraphs detailing the workings of the Sanhedrin, with at least two whole tractates of the Talmud of elaboration, that these are all meaningless, because we have this single article 3, item 10 in Maimonides which nixes all of it? This is Klinghoffer's view.

I'm sure Maimonides himself would be terribly perplexed to see how his work is being manipulated here.

Klinghoffer would have better made his point regarding the king's alternative sentencing had he stopped there and hadn't felt obliged to add on more proof. (Perhaps he himself found his evidence unbalanced.)

King David himself availed himself of these provisions on at least two occasions (2 Samuel 1:15, 4:9).

Perhaps we should start by reading how Samuel felt about installing a king in the first place:

> "Is it not wheat harvest to-day? I will call unto God, that He may send thunder and rain; and you shall know and see that your wickedness is great, which you have done in the sight of God, in asking you a king." So Samuel called unto God; and God sent thunder and rain that day; and all the people greatly feared God and Samuel. And all the people said unto Samuel: "Pray for thy servants unto the Lord your God, that we not die; for we have added unto all our sins this evil, to ask us a king." (1 Samuel 12:17-19)

Following those impressive special effects, Samuel consents to give the people the king they wanted, but he—and God—are clearly disappointed and, historically, this moment marks the beginning of the end of the Jewish experiment in tribal co-existence under Torah Law. The rest of our national history is a succession of failures of our kings to reach the prophetic heights envisioned by Moses and Samuel.

The first citation Klinghoffer brings to prove that David availed himself of the Maimonidean permission, 2 Samuel 1:15, tells of the battlefield incident where an Amalekite youth proclaimed that he had killed King Saul, and David, shocked, orders the youth killed.

Except that David was not yet the ruling king! Yes, he had been anointed by the prophet Samuel, and he had a large following from his tribe of Judea, but 2 Samuel proceeds for several more chapters to detail David's difficult path to the crown.

If we were to examine this story as an example of the king's broad judiciary powers as delineated by Maimonides, where is the evidence of even an attempt at a court proceeding? For one thing, there was no testimony, since Jewish law does not permit individuals to incriminate themselves (*ein adam mesim atzmo rasha*). So this was not, as in Maimonides' proposition, a faulty procedure which utilizes the king's status to make it legal, but rather a battlefield stroke which did not require any judicial process at all.

In the second verse Klinghoffer cites, David metes out a similar punishment to the murderers of his dead dear friend Jonathan's handicapped heir (2 Samuel 4:9). Again, this happens well before David is accepted widely as the king, and we see no evidence of a faulty trial which the king's authority legitimizes.

Both of these are really cases of the king settling personal scores— not a king acting to fix a broken legal system.

Klinghoffer conveniently avoids discussing the most famous misuse of executive power, when David falls in love with a married woman, Bat Sheba. David sends her husband Uriah to be killed in battle and takes the woman for himself.

There isn't in the entire Bible a more compelling case for the need to limit the king's powers, and David is rebuked sternly by the Prophet Nathan and is eventually punished many times over by God (start at 2 Samuel 11 and just keep going).

If only we could arrange for the prophet Nathan to bring Dick Cheney in for a conversation about executive privilege....

But Klinghoffer doesn't just read Maimonides as preferring the executive short cut to the Torah ideal; he further commits the sin of misleading about the sources. This is serious stuff. He suggests the Jewish king is permitted to execute an accused based not only on incomplete testimony as described above, but on "circumstantial evidence, as in an American court."

He suggests the proof for this astonishing assertion is in Maimonides' *Guide to the Perplexed* (3:40). You know he's turning on the smoke and mirrors when he adds sheepishly: *Not that the matter is simple...*

Remember the Beheaded Heifer? In Part 3 of his *Guide*, Maimonides offers common sense reasons to a long list of divine commandments, under the proviso that the real reason we keep them is because God said so, but, still, we should strive to understand the value of each commandment in improving our spiritual and physical lives. In the last paragraph of Chapter 40 in Part 3, he deals with the commandment of the beheaded heifer.

Maimonides asks: Why do we create this great fanfare, get the elderly judges out to the riverbank to measure the distances and then engage in this brutal ceremony? Then he answers: To generate public interest, so that people will start talking about the case and the discussion will lead a witness to appear..

Maimonides' view is that ignoring an actual murderer is a grave sin in itself. For the sake of preventing this sin, he suggests that even a woman, even a handmaiden, may come up with testimony about the real murderer—and that even circumstantial evidence is valid, because the king can come forward and legitimize the process and execute the newly discovered suspect.

This is a creative and imaginative idea, which Maimonides kept to himself and to the small circle of learned scholars he envisioned as his target audience in the *Guide*, as opposed to his *Mishneh Torah* which was intended for wide dissemination.

Maimonides never dreamed of including this notion as part of the law, nor did he intend for it to be used outside the scope of the case of a corpse which is found near a town.

To extrapolate from that hidden and private notion a broad assumption about the use of circumstantial evidence *in an American court* is dishonest in the extreme.

Where Maimonides would bend the law to execute a guilty murderer, Klinghoffer would break it to execute an innocent man!

I opened this chapter with a musing about Klinghoffer's objection to Yeshiva's Innocence Project as an example of sissy Orthodox Jews "buckling under pressure" rather than applauding the execution of dozens of innocents as he believes they ought to. I was bewildered by his absence of enthusiasm at the prospect of Jewish students pursuing justice. It bothered me especially because I support the principle of the death penalty and would like to see it be restored. In this light, it's worth noting how many of these wrongful convictions would have been avoided had the standards of Jewish law been followed by American courts.

According to the Innocence Project,[1] "Limited, unreliable or fraudulent forensic science"—that is to say, circumstantial evidence—"has played a role in 65 percent of wrongful convictions."

Jewish law does not allow confessions to count as testimony. The legal reasoning is simple: If the confession is true, how can we rely on the word of a criminal? This bedrock principal of Jewish jurisprudence also prevents the occurrence of something the Inquisition discovered centuries later: Proper application of force can make a man confess to anything.

So it is not surprising that 25 percent of the cases where innocence was proven post-conviction involved false confessions and incriminating statements.

Finally, snitches contributed to wrongful convictions in 15 percent of cases. Putting aside the common sense that dictates that such testimony is often tainted because it is offered in exchange for special treatment, or the dropping of charges. The simple fact in Jewish law is that jail-house snitches are generally criminals—and are therefore disqualified as witnesses.

If a court that executes once in 70 years is "murderous," what can be said of Klinghoffer's deeply un-Jewish blood lust that can be sated with the blood of innocents? His desire for the death penalty is certainly at odds with his general ideology.

---

[1]   "Facts on Post-Conviction DNA Exonerations" retrieved from http://www.innocenceproject.org/Content/351.php on July 24, 2008.

He doesn't trust government to heal the sick, nurture the elderly, teach the young, manage the markets, regulate drugs, inspect food and on and on. In all those areas government is untrustworthy, self-promoting, corrupt, inept.

But when it comes to cops, lawyers, juries and judges putting people to death, all of his doubts dissipate and Klinghoffer is filled with a wide-eyed acceptance of government's competence and incorruptibility.

Does he simply trust anyone armed with a gun or an electric chair? Or does Klinghoffer simply relish the death of the executed? Where Maimonides would bend the law to execute a guilty murder, Klinghoffer would break it to execute an innocent man!

11

Warrantless Research:
Klinghoffer's Spy Game

American readers of Klinghoffer's chapter 14, "Privacy: I Spy?" will be glad to know that the power to approve wiretapping warrants invested in the United States Foreign Intelligence Surveillance Court by the 1978 Foreign Intelligence Surveillance Act (FISA) do not violate the Torah. Even the controversial expanded eavesdropping powers handed George W. Bush by a supine Congress in the summer of 2008 do not violate the broad constitutional outlines of the Torah.

No one ever said they did.

But that didn't stop Klinghoffer from publishing an earlier version of this chapter in a national Jewish magazine, thereby pulling off one of the most brazen pieces of Jewish conservative propaganda in an era filled with them.

In defending only the defensible portion of the spying and wiretapping practices, (and avoiding discussion of the *indefensible* ones) Klinghoffer's implicit argument is that all the tussles between civil liberties groups and the Republican administration have been misdirected rubbish—a tempest in a teapot.

That, of course, is not the case.

The issue is still obscured by secrecy. Hints of the illegality of the Bush Administration's spying activities directed against Americans arose in 2005, when *The New York Times* reported that:

> Months after the Sept. 11 attacks, President Bush secretly authorized the National Security Agency to eavesdrop on Americans and others inside the United States to search for evidence of terrorist activity without the court-approved warrants ordinarily required for domestic spying, according to government officials.
>
> Under a presidential order signed in 2002, the intelligence agency has monitored the international telephone calls and international e-mail messages of hundreds, perhaps thousands, of people inside the United States without warrants over the past three years....

As the years went on, more details were revealed.

For one thing, acting Attorney General James B. Comey found the spying program so illegal that in 2004 he refused to sign an authorization for the NSA program, saying it "did not comply with the law." Attorney General John Ashcroft, F.B.I. Director Robert S. Mueller III, and other senior Justice Department aides all threatened to resign over the program's illegalities.

Whatever this program was, it wasn't spying on foreigners overseas, as the administration repeatedly insisted was their goal, and as is the case in the scenario Klinghoffer describes.

That was *already allowed* under the FISA law—which in any case the administration didn't feel bound by.

Under their doctrine of expanded war powers, the Bush Administration claimed they could do anything necessary in the name of the war on terror—including jailing American citizens forever, without access to a court system.

Nobody is arguing that the Bush Administration acted against the Torah. Just that it has acted illegally, unconstitutionally and, in its appeal to the untrammeled executive powers, in a profoundly un-American fashion.

(Klinghoffer's appeal on Bush's behalf to the examples of Solomon and the Maimonidean notion of untrammeled executive powers drive home the point. As Klinghoffer may have forgotten, with all due respect to the Scriptures, the prime directive of American democracy is the rejection of kings and all their trappings.)

So what *is* against the Torah? Lying.

Even lying by omission or misdirection.

That's called *gneivat da'at*—mental theft. It's creating thoughts and ideas deceitfully, and it's as wrong as creating wealth and money deceitfully.

And it's exactly what Klinghoffer has done in this essay, designed to make readers think Bush acted in a way that he didn't, and that civil liberties supporters argued something that they didn't. From the Torah's standpoint, *Klinghoffer* is the scofflaw.

In this case, from the standpoint of *halacha* (Jewish Law), Klinghoffer's coverup is clearly worse than Bush's crime.

12

This is a Conservative on Drugs

Out of David Klinghoffer's entire opus, his chapter on drugs and drug policy is easily the least coherent and the most embarrassing. If in other chapters he makes an actual effort to build a case—albeit faulty—for this or that Conservative view, here he gives up all pretense and goes with the tried and true "Because I said so!" And the less coherent he becomes, the further he flies into a fantasy realm all his own, giving up even the feeblest claim that any of this drivel is based in Jewish tradition.

His central theme in this chapter is that

> [W]e are right to make clear distinction between substances like cocaine and marijuana on one hand, and cigarettes and alcohol on the other.[1]

---
[1] Klinghoffer, p.168.

Moreover,

> in a biblical-constitutional regime, the war on drugs
> would go on, while the crusade against cigarettes
> would be lifted.[2]

I can think of only two distinctions between cigarettes and alcohol on the one hand and all the rest of the recreational drugs on the other: the amount of damage they cause to life and property, and better lobbyists.

The number one killer in the United States for many decades has been Tobacco, with 435,000 annual deaths[3]. Next comes Poor Diet and Physical Inactivity: 365,000, and in third place Alcohol: 85,000.

The only "drugs" to register on this list are "Anti-Inflammatory Drugs Such As Aspirin," which kill 7,600 annually.

Marijuana, hashish, cocaine, heroine, LSD, and mixes like Methamphetamine, combined, don't produce enough deaths to register on the list of top ten killers. Indeed, typically, deaths associated with these and similar substances are most often the result of their illegality, which results in murderous turf wars among dealers, and deaths from badly cooked, unregulated product.

But this is not an article advocating drug legalization; it's only a critique of Klinghoffer's manhandling of scripture. So, you wish to know why he promotes leaving alone the killer of nearly half a million Americans every year, while revving up the war on drugs? To tell you the truth, it's hard to say. At first glance, it appears that he actually bases his entire thesis on an idiotic reading of scripture. On a second glance, it turns out he really is basing the whole thing on an idiotic reading of scripture.

---

[2] Klinghoffer, p.168.

[3]   "Actual Causes of Death in the United States, 2000," *Journal of the American Medical Association*, March 10, 2004, Vol. 291, No. 10.

Here's what happened: It was a very exciting occasion for the Israelites in the wilderness. After months of constructing the Tent of Ap-
pointment, their first version of the Temple, the day came to offer their
first sacrifices there.

> And Moses and Aaron went into the tent of appointment,
> and came out, and blessed the people; and the glory of God
> appeared before all the people. And there came forth fire from
> before God, and consumed upon the altar the burnt-offering
> and the fat; and when all the people saw it, they shouted, and
> fell on their faces. [Lev. 9:23-4]

So far, so good. But then, the two sons of Aaron, the High Priest,
became overexcited and suffered terrible consequences:

> And Nadab and Abihu, the sons of Aaron, took each of
> them his censer, and put fire therein, and laid incense thereon,
> and offered foreign fire before God, which He had not com-
> manded them. And there came forth fire from before God,
> and devoured them, and they died before God. [Lev. 10:1-2]

Generations of commentators have elaborated on this passage, each
offering his exciting take, but the bottom line, the direct, simple, un-
disputed meaning (the *poshut pshat*) is that our priests were barred from
adding of their own resources to the prescribed ritual, and by doing so
they blasphemed.

Klinghoffer bases much of his anti-drug argument on the above passage. You want to know how he got there? With a lot of elbowing…

> According to tradition, the fire entered their nostrils,
> incinerating their bodies, while leaving their clothing
> intact. In the Bible, the punishment always fits the
> crime; so the fact that the fire entered their noses to
> kill them would suggest that in their sin, they ingested

something through the same organ. I'm not saying they snorted cocaine, but a certain echo is there.[4]

As a joke in an email, perhaps this rubbish has some legitimacy. As an argument on which to balance an entire theory this is seriously embarrassing. I kept reading on, waiting for a clever punchline, something to show me that he didn't really mean to come across this challenged, but I had to admit, as the immortal Groucho Marx put it in *Duck Soup:* "Chicolini here may talk like an idiot and look like an idiot, but don't let that fool you, he really *is* an idiot!"

Where did Klinghoffer get the fire in the nose image? Rashi on Lev. 10:5 cites tractate Sanhedrin 52b:

Abba Yossi b. Dostai says: Two threads of fire came out from the holiest sanctuary, and were divided into four, and entered each two in each one's nose, and burned them.

So, first of all, it isn't the Bible that suggests the sons' death was an example of diving poetic justice, it's a Talmudic sage, within the context of an entirely different issue (the qualities of execution by burning). There certainly is a suggestion, made by the Talmud and many commentators, that the fact that the prohibition on priestly inebriation appears a scant few verses later, can be taken to mean that Nadab's and Abihu's sin stemmed from their drunkenness. But if they were drunk, how does Klinghoffer come up with the snorting thing? What "certain echo" is there, for heaven's sake?

The reason our sages were troubled by the idea of God's burning the two sons has to do with a major principle in executing the condemned under Jewish law: Since man was created in God's image, we are not permitted to alter the appearance of the body through the execution process, lest we cause God's image to appear grotesque. This may also be one of the reasons we hurry to bury the dead, before decomposi-

---

[4] Klinghoffer, p.169.

tion sets in This is also the reason why our method of burning the condemned is by making them ingest molten led, so that their outside remains intact. But if God burned the bodies, didn't that desecrate them? To which Rabbi Yossi b. Dostai replies, He burned their insides, leaving the body intact.

It wasn't about sniffing anything, it was about seeking consistency in Jewish law. But consistency on drug policy is as foreign to Klinghoffer as the fire brought in by Aaron's children. Because you have to ask yourself, if the one substance being depicted in Leviticus 10 as the possible reason for the sin of Aaron's sons is wine, why does Klinghoffer lump alcohol with cigarettes as good substances, while declaring marijuana, hashish and the rest bad?

It's very hard to follow why he's against a ban on smoking and in favor of a ban on "bad" drugs. He is very upset with his home state of Washington's severe anti-smoking policies, declaring this to be yet another case of liberals discounting "the ability of adults to make responsible choices." He admits that smoking is a dangerous habit, and spending "lots of time around heavy smokers is also unhealthy." But somehow he finds fault in government's seeking to protect office workers and restaurant diners from taking in a dose of their neighbors' lung pollution.

Klinghoffer's "biblical democracy" (a term replete with internal contradiction, much like his "Judeo-Christian" delusion) "would be wary of banning tobacco cigarettes if only to make clear society's commitment to the idea of personal responsibility."

It is interesting to regard an addiction so debilitating that it robs men and women of their mobility, their voices, and, finally, their very ability to breathe—and still many continue to sneak a smoke even in their cancer ward beds—as being given to choice and "personal responsibility." Klinghoffer's pretense that the addict can just say "No" is astonishing. His attempt to include the Bible in this medley of cruelty and blindness lands him on a path to yet more bizarre stuff.

For instance, having made his strong case in favor of letting people make their own choices regarding their bad habits, he states: "All this analysis, however, has to be turned on its head when we switch our focus from cigarettes to mind-altering drugs." In other words, if you smoke tobacco you are a responsible adult, but when you switch to weed, all that responsibility just goes out the window. Except that this really gets funny, because—as Klinghoffer himself puts it—we have no evidence of what the Bible has to say about those mind altering drugs, because "the Bible discusses only alcohol explicitly."

You have to pay attention here, as this is going to be one heck of a sleight of hand. Klinghoffer is going to attempt to extract an anti-drug view from the Bible using only verses that deal with wine, and then conclude that wine itself is a good substance, and that his Biblical America "needs wine and, it would seem, plenty of it."

This is one death defying trick, reminiscent of the amazing Supreme Court decision of December, 2000, when a court which for decades had waved the banner of states' rights, decided in a late-night gathering to kill the Florida court's decision regarding ballot counting, and then proceeded to declare this a one-time only decision, never again to be repeated for the benefit of, say, a Democrat.

So try and follow the magician's quick fingers in slow motion:

Klinghoffer brings a minority opinion in the Talmud, according to which the Tree of Knowledge was a grapevine (the other options include wheat and fig—the apple idea may have been pure Botticelli). Having taken that direction, he now proceeds to alter the very essence of the sin of Adam and Eve.

Our classical notion of the sin of *Gan Eden* is that it was a violation of God's will (Nahmanides, Gen. 3:13). God owned the garden and by heeding His decree not to eat from that tree, Adam and Eve would have recognized His ownership over everything, this, ultimately, being humanity's mission.

But Klinghoffer has a more practical explanation: It was because they got high. This is no longer an epic story of humanity's failure to acknowledge God the Ruler of the Universe; instead it's a tale of two junkies.

It's not such a terrible idea, particularly if you share it with your fellow sufferers at an AA meeting. But Klinghoffer can't stop there. Remember, he can't just prove that Adam and Eve sinned by drinking wine—he has to beat those grapes into mushrooms. So he comes up with the following pearl, arguably the strangest statement in his entire book:

> The Bible thus indicates to us the main danger of consciousness-altering substances. They hold out the hope of forcing a unity between people and God. More generally, a point that comes out in a variety of later biblical teachings, they fill our minds with illusions and untruths.[5]

You have to admire the way he substituted "consciousness-altering substances" for wine. That's the only way to sneak in those pesky drugs, because, obviously, there's no mention of them anywhere in the Bible or, for that matter, in any Jewish source earlier than the mid-to-late 20th Century. The scant discussions of drugs among Talmudic and medieval sages is only in a medical context (with one cute exception that Klinghoffer's Judaica CD ROM doesn't offer, or he surely would have cited it).

But forget about the tricks – do you realize Klinghoffer's message here? He's painting in negative terms the very notion of man's yearning to get close to God. It's an illusion, born by hallucinatory wine (the bad kind).

But if that's the case, what is the experience of prophecy, then? Is it not an attempt to get close to God? And isn't it a mind-altering experience?

> And the spirit of God will come mightily upon you, and you will prophesy with them, and will be turned into another man. [I Sam. 18:10]

---

[5] Klinghoffer, p.172.

In their chapter on ecstasy in the *Encyclopedia Judaica*, Shalom M. Paul and S. David Sperling suggest that prophets would "fall into an ecstatic trance, like Elijah who ran before Ahab's chariot when the hand of the Lord was upon him (I Kings 18:46)." They add:

> This is doubtless why a disciple of the prophets is referred to as "the madman" (II Kings 9:11). But a careful reading of the classical prophets shows that they too manifested odd behavior. Jeremiah is referred to as "madman" and "ecstatic" (mitnabbe) in the same breath (Jer. 29:26; cf. Hos. 9:7). Isaiah walked about barefoot and naked for three years (Isa. 20:3). Ezekiel lay on his left side for 390 days and 40 days on his right. From Zech. 13:4–6 we learn that a prophet might be expected to wear a hairshirt and have sores on his back, perhaps from some ritual beating. Indeed, the Hebrew word for madman, meshugga, may be a terminus technicus for a type of god-inspired individual... Such an ecstatic seizure may be induced by external means: music (cf. Elisha, II Kings 3:15, and the musical instruments carried by the bands of prophets, I Sam. 10:5 and II Chron. 35:15)...

This ecstatic behavior is inseparable from prophetic inspiration. It is also part of the process of seeking contact with the Divine:

> All the prophets do not prophecy whenever they want, but they must direct their minds and sit in contentment (*smechim v'tovey lev*) and in isolation, since prophecy does not inspire in a state of sadness, nor sloth, only in contentment, therefore the disciples of the prophets play for them on harp, drum, flute and violin while they seek prophecy.... [Maimonides, *Hilchot Yesodei Torah*, 7:4]

The state of *simcha*, which Maimonides and others do not read as joy, but as contentment, is essential to all encounters with the Divine, including that of the High Priest—who comes in direct contact with the Divine on Yom Kippur. The prerequisites for both prophets and priests include being married, having children, having wealth and being in a state of *simcha*.

The psalmist offers the classical endorsement of a rapid access to such a state:

> And wine gladdens (*yesamach*) the heart of man, making his face cheerful as if it were daubed with oil, and bread that feeds man's heart. [Psalms 104:15]

So, in order to justify the failed US War on Drugs, Klinghoffer is prepared to deny the fundamentals of divine inspiration and prophecy. He actually writes:

> Adam and Eve were only the first to fantasize that they could be one with the ultimate *other*, the ultimate One, God. Most drug users and drunks just want a quick way to relax social inhibitions. But the really perilous promise held out by these substances is a blasphemy: the identification of the self with God.[6]

Down the drain go three thousand years of Jewish yearnings to follow in the footsteps of our grandfather Jacob, who fought with God's angel, forcing the latter to bless him: "Your name shall be called no more Jacob, but Israel; for you have strived with God and with men, and prevailed. [Gen. 32:29]" No good, according to Klinghoffer, blasphemy. You can't be like God, even if God said so. Why? Because then I'll lose the culture war between potheads and Republicans. Something like that...

How does Klinghoffer conclude his misinformed fiasco? How does he resurrect the legitimacy of wine, after having used it in example after

---

[6] Klinghoffer, p.174.

example as the representative of all the evil, mind-altering substances? By saying so:

> Simply, alcohol is the exception that proves the rule....

and

> It would be impossible to fully observe the Bible's commandments if you never drank wine....

and

> "rejoicing" being commanded for the festival day can refer only to drinking wine.[7]

Simply. Alcohol is apparently like a red heifer, which cleanses the impure but sullies the pure. Having done its job as the paradigm for all the worst mind-altering substances in the world, wine can now retreat quietly and be consumed safely, having forever condemned those evil reefers, because it's the exception that proves the rule. How did it prove the rule and why it's the exception need not be explained. If you were a conservative, you'd know.

This is the fourth chapter I've had the dubious pleasure of responding to in Klinghoffer's book, and it is by far the least intelligent. Worse, it's quite clear that the author is painfully aware of the logical morass through which he's dragging his reader, stating this fact shamelessly several times along the way. In the end, his "common sense" rests safely on the same shelf with "because I said so." But then again, if it all comes down to "because I said so," he could make it a much shorter book, possibly with fun drawings.

Cheers!

---

[7] Klinghoffer, p.175-6.

13

War: Klinghoffer's Pope Urban Renewal

When Klinghoffer turns his attention to war, it's tempting to ask him: Would God have voted to authorize the war with Iraq?

Given that God would have known the consequences of the war; the false premises under which it was being sold to the American people; and the truth that Saddam Hussein was not an imminent danger to America, and if anything was providing a counterbalance to Iran, one would suspect that God would not have.

But the real question is, given the principles that God has given us, how should our non-omniscient representatives in Congress have voted?

Klinghoffer deflects this question by arguing another point entirely: absolute pacifism is not Biblically correct.

If this were a Christian book, it might be worth debating that point. Are the Quakers right that non-violence is the only Christian solution? Was Methodist leader Jim Winkler correct that Jesus did not support the war in Iraq? Does "Blessed are the peacemakers, for they shall be called sons of God (Matthew 5:9) apply to international relations? None of my business.

But even as Klinghoffer defends the Bush administration's rush to war by fighting the pacifist straw man, he's demonstrating something real about the conservative approach to warfare.

After discussing the Christian tradition of pacifism, Klinghoffer cites approvingly "the concept of *kerygma*, warfare justified on the grounds that it spread the gospel to unbelievers – we might call it 'holy war,' or perhaps *jihad*."[1]

Klinghoffer goes on to praise the "farsighted Pope Urban,"[2] who declared holy war against the Muslims in 1095. The First Crusade, Klinghoffer assures us, "was defensive in nature." Furthermore, "When Pope Urban commissioned his crusaders, he also did so by offering to them the example of Moses."[3] By this view, both Church and Torah agree that war can be good.

At this point, knowledgeable Jews won't believe that I'm quoting Klinghoffer fairly. Because for Jewish memory, the Crusades were not simply an example of religiously motivated warfare; they were a catastrophe. They were not a model to be emulated. Reports the *Encyclopedia Judaica*:

> In the memory of the Jews, the Crusades became the symbol of the opposition between Christianity an Judaism. Historians believe that the semi-mourning that marks the period between Passover and Shavuot reflects the events of 1096.

---

[1] Klinghoffer, p.201.
[2] Klinghoffer, p.202.
[3] Klinghoffer, p.204.

Here is what happened when a gang of crusaders, inspired by the enthusiasm sparked by Pope Urban's call for jihad, reached the city of Worms, one of the largest Jewish communities in what we now call Germany:

> "The crusaders first massacred the Jews who had re-mained in their houses, then, eight days later, those who had sought an illusory refuge in the bishop's castle. The victims numbered about 800; only a few accepted conversion and survived, the great majority choosing to be killed or suicide rather than apostasy. Hearing of the massacre, the Jews of Mains asked for the bishop's protection, paying him 400 pieces of silver to this end. When the crusaders, led by [Count] Emicho, arrived outside the town on the third of Sivan (May 27, 1096), the burghers hastened to open the gates. The Jews took up arms under the leadership of Kalonymus b. Meshullam. Weakened through fasting, for they had hoped to avert the disaster through exemplary piety, the Jews had to retreat to the bishop's castle; how-ever the latter could do nothing for them, as he himself had to flee before the combined assault of crusaders and burghers. After a brief struggle, a wholesale mas-sacre ensued. More than 1,000 Jews met their deaths, either at the enemy's hands or their own. Those who managed to escape were overtaken; almost no one sur-vived. A comparable disaster occurred in Cologne.... At Regensburg, all the Jews were dragged to the Dan-ube where they were flung into the water and forced to accept baptism. At Metz, Prague, and throughout Bohemia, one massacre followed another."

By the time the crusaders were stopped (by Hungarian Christians),

"There had been more than 5,000 victims."

Klinghoffer gleefully quotes a Crusader chronicle that when they sacked Jerusalem—after declining to accept a truce which would guarantee the rights of Christian pilgrims—the Christians stood with "blood up to their knees and bridle reins."[4]

Klinghoffer doesn't mention the chronicle of Ibn al-Qalanisi which states the Jewish defenders sought refuge in their synagogue, but the "Franks burned it over their heads," killing everyone inside. The Crusaders circled the flaming building while singing "Christ, We Adore Thee!"

So what do we learn from all this—besides the obvious fact that Klinghoffer has been blinded by his lust for Muslim blood?

How might a fuller picture of the Crusades inform how we should have thought about invading Iraq?

One answer is that wars have consequences that may be unintended —but can nonetheless be expected. As the *Judaica* relates, "At the outset, nothing in the proclamation of Urban II seemed to threaten the Jews, but it would appear that the Jews in France sensed danger, since they sent emissaries to the Rhine communities to warn them of the possible threat."

So too, emissaries were sent to warn the Bush Administration of the possible threats posed by invading Iraq. But just as Klinghoffer is too blinded by his desire for a pure "holy war" to remember the Jewish martyrs (whose laments are still recited by traditional Jews every summer), George Bush, Dick Cheney and Donald Rumsfeld were so excited by their desire for a war that they ignored predictable consequences.

There was no planning for an occupation.

"We didn't go in with a plan. We went in with a theory," a veteran State Department official told Knight-Ridder newspapers.[5]

How to explain this lack of forethought?

---

[4] Klinghoffer, p.202.

[5]   http://www.commondreams.org/headlines04/1016-06.htm

The example of Klinghoffer suggests an answer.

Like Klinghoffer, and perhaps like Pope Urban, the Bush Administration decision makers were blinded by ideology. Their lust for war with Iraq did not reflect a pragmatic responses to the threat of Iraqi nuclear weapons. (If it had been, they wouldn't have had to propagate what they knew to be misleading descriptions of Iraq's nuclear program, even while not giving weapons inspectors a chance to look for weapons.) Convinced of their ideology, and perhaps under the influence of religious ideologues like Klinghoffer who would conflate neoconservative political theory with Divine Will, there was no reason to look for facts, examine the evidence, or even try to tell American people the whole truth.

Amalek today?

It's worth contrasting how Pope Urban—and by extension Klinghoffer—use the Biblical story of Amalek with how the Talmudic sages treat it. For Urban and Klinghoffer, the command to war with Amalek is the model for a holy war against the enemies of God.

Yet for the Talmud the war is now only hypothetical. The Biblical kingdom of Amalek, like Moab and Ammon no longer exist:[6]

> Sennacherib king of Assyria long ago went up and mixed up all the nations, as it says, "I have removed the bounds of the peoples and have robbed their treasures and have brought down as one mighty their inhabitants."[7]

The wars the Torah commanded Jews to wage and the grudges we were commanded to keep have expired. At the simplest level, the Tal-

---

[6]   For a more detailed discussion of this and other rabbinic passages regarding Amalek, see Helfgot, Nathaniel, "Amalek: Ethics, Values and Halakhic Development" in Helfgot, Nathaniel, ed., *The Yeshivat Chovevei Torah Rabbinical School Tanakh Companion to the Book of Samuel*, Teaneck: Ben Yehuda Press 2006.

[7]   Talmud Berachot 28a, quoting Isaiah 10:13

mud is saying that the geopolitical order has changed. It's not enough to fight the people who live where Amalek used to live; one can't revenge the destruction of the Temple by the Babylonians by fighting the Iraqi, or the sack of the Temple by the Romans by fighting the Italians. There is, after all, a limit to keeping grudges.

On a more subtle level, however, I think the Talmud is making a very deep point about war and revenge. Sennacherib, who exiled ten tribes and almost destroyed Jerusalem, marked the beginning of a different kind of warfare in Jewish history. The period of Israel's conquests was long past; the beginning of Israel as a victim of imperial forces was at hand.

If, in the early Biblical history Israel's victory or defeat reflected its moral worth or not, that was hardly the case in the Rabbinic response to Jewish decimation at the hands of the Roman empire, or the later millennium of European Christian oppression, which began with Pope Urban and ended with Adolph Hitler. In these times, war is war, and war is hell, hints the Talmud; empires and their wars sweep aside whole nations, guilty and innocent alike.

Thus, while it may be rhetorically useful to equate an enemy with Amalek, that is not an approach the Talmud follows.

Klinghoffer alludes to an important Talmudic rule for warfare, one codified by Maimonides: The king, for a "war of choice," must receive the approval of the Sanhedrin, the equivalent of the legislature.

Maimonides didn't contemplate the king perjuring himself to the Sanhedrin.

But that's what happened in America. Intelligence was cherry picked. Congress was presented with information that the administration knew not to be reliable—but which made the case it wanted to make.

Indeed, author Craig Unger suggests that officials connected with the Bush administration were working to instigate war with Iraq even before Bush was inaugurated, stealing stationery from the Niger embassy in Italy which was used to forge documents later used as evidence that Iraq sought to obtain uranium.[8]

So how should have a congressman who wanted to know how God really would vote?

Certainly they should have applied deliberation to debate. After all, the hallmark of the Sanhedrin was learned debate. (Remember: On a capital case, the Sanhedrin couldn't convict unless the acquittal side had convinced at least one judge.)

And they would have applied the lesson of Jewish history: Excessive enthusiasm for a crusade is at least as dangerous to all concerned as is principled pacifism.

---

[8]   Unger, Craig, *The Fall of the House of Bush: The Untold Story of How a Band of True Believers Seized the Executive Branch, Started the Iraq War, and Still Imperils America's Future*, Scribner 2007.

14

Is David Klinghoffer Jewish?

Here's a radical question for you: Is David Klinghoffer Jewish?

I don't want to question his personal history, so let me rephrase that: Is David Klinghoffer a Jewish thinker? Or is he a Jew who operates in a non-Jewish intellectual mode? Someone like, say, Noam Chomsky or Karl Marx?

Klinghoffer presents himself as an Orthodox Jew, bringing Jewish insights to a conservative evangelical Christian audience.

But does he really have a Jewish soul? Does he exhibit a healthy sense of self-preservation on behalf of his people? Does he feel threatened if any Jew—even one he disagrees with—is threatened?

As we've seen throughout this book, there is ample evidence that Klinghoffer isn't Jewish—at least not where it counts, in his *kishkes*.

He lacks Jewish historical memory.

At key junctures, he chooses Pauline theology over Rabbinic theology.

And he evinces a shocking willingness to sell out fellow Jews wholesale for the apparent amusement of his Christian audience.

This last charge is in some ways the least, so let's start with it.

On page 10, he describes the Anti-Defamation League as "a group that is Jewish only in the sense that bagels are Jewish."

Klinghoffer is being more perceptive than he realizes.

Because where most people understand bagels to be simply rolls victimized by a sloppy circumcision, Klinghoffer understands that bagels were created, like the ADL, "to stop the defamation of the Jewish people and to secure justice and fair treatment to all."

Indeed, bagels are today the premiere carbohydrate "fighting anti-Semitism through programs and services that counteract hatred, prejudice and bigotry," a function performed in the organizational realm by the ADL.

Klinghoffer's problem with the ADL is that it fights bigotry—and he wants his religion served up with nice fat shmears of hatred.

A word about contemporary Christian and conservative anti-Semitism. It seems that it is now okay in the circles Klinghoffer travels in to traffic in traditional anti-Semitic stereotypes—such as Jewish control of Hollywood—if you distinguish between evil, "secular" Jews and good, religious Jews. Jews such as, ahem, David Klinghoffer.

I received a first-hand introduction to this world of anti-Semitism a couple of years ago, when I idly tuned my radio to the AM dial. In the course of this random 15 minute listen[1], I was shocked at the vehemence with which "secular Jews" were being labeled as "the enemy." This was classical anti-Semitism being stoked by the talk show host, and it was apparently kosher because it was only "liberal" Jews who

---

[1]   Admittedly, it's possible that I tuned in to a one-time example of such hatred. However, given Klinghoffer's willingness to generalize from personal experience (cf. his proof that the Bible is a conservative document, which is: "I have never met one, not one individual, who as a result of becoming more engaged with the Bible became more politically liberal") I feel I'm on safe ground here.

were being attacked. That is to say, some of the host's best friends, as it were, were religious Jews.

In other words, conservative "right-thinking," religious Jews like Klinghoffer were giving cover for anti-Semites to blame the country's problems on a Jewish conspiracy.

It's simply not "Jewish" to feel safe while *any* Jew is being attacked. Jews know that when push comes to shove, distinctions fall away. Any attack on Jews is an attack on every Jew. The Jewish community is one.

Klinghoffer cares more for his religion of bigotry than he does for his fellow Jews with whom he disagrees. That's why he can't stand the ADL, which occasionally calls him and his allies on their misbehavior.

Klinghoffer engages in one of the gravest of Jewish sins, separating oneself from the Jewish community to become the beneficiary of gentile largess.

As long as he is free to disbelieve in Jesus, he doesn't care what happens to other Jews.

How else to explain his deafness to the cries of his brother's blood, that calls out from the history of the crusades that Klinghoffer praises?

When Klinghoffer dismisses the slaughter of Jewish communities in 1096 as an unfortunate accident in the necessary defense of Europe from the Muslim East—when he revels in Muslim blood spilt in Jerusalem but doesn't smell the smoke of Jews burnt in their synagogue by the Christian crusaders—whose side is he on? Hasn't he taken up the Cross, not only against the Crescent, but against the Jewish people?

Why does he defend Pope Urban and his Church? Does he hate Islam too harshly, embrace Christendom too ardently, or love Jews too little?

Or take his praise, on page 16, for a 19th century New York court ruling disallowing testimony from an atheist. Klinghoffer seems to have forgotten—or never known—that until five years earlier, Jews were denied political rights by the constitution of the State of Maryland, which stated that "all persons professing the Christian religion are equally entitled to protection in their religious liberty." So while Klinghoffer pines for the good old days of the 19th century, when American liberties were not extended to atheists, he lacks the Jewish *kishke* which would note that the liberties not extended to atheists were only hesitantly extended to Jews.

There's a reason why the ADL opposes all bigotry. It's the same reason the American Jewish Committee aligned itself with the National Association for the Advancement of Colored People. It's because a world where bigotry has no sanction is a world infinitely safer for the Jews.

What became clear listening to conservative talk radio, and more recently reading conservative writings, is how deeply ingrained, and how vastly acceptable, hatred has become in American discourse.

It's OK to hope that San Francisco is leveled with an earthquake, to wish that a terrorist attacked The New York Times building, to dismiss entire states as "un-American."

As a Jew, I know that a rising tide of hatred swamps all boats.

And to the extent that Klinghoffer helps make bigoted Christians feel better about their bigotry, I can't help feeling that he has made my life in America—and that of my children—more precarious.

Klinghoffer's professed "non-Zionism" is also telling.

He's annoyed that all the talk about Israel—about the physical well-being of half the world's Jews—occupies media that could otherwise be sharing the Torah's (which is to say, Klinghoffer's) views of how to arrange the world. In seeking to engage and confront the wider world, Klinghoffer is indeed venturing on the "modern Orthodox" path paved by Rabbi Samson Raphael Hirsch in the early 19th century. But the 20th century's leading modern Orthodox sage, Rabbi Joseph B. Soloveitchik, departed from the Hirschian path and embraced Zionism, putting the question of Jewish physical survival on an equal plane to the propagation of Torah.

Klinghoffer, alas, fails to understand why, and thereby shows how he, unlike Rav Soloveitchik, remains unaffected by the Holocaust.

For Rav Soloveitchik, the lesson of the Holocaust and the creation of the State of Israel was that the Divine covenant with the Jewish people was twofold: There was a "covenant of faith," constituting the revelation of the Torah at Sinai. And there was the earlier "covenant of fate," which God made with Abraham, Isaac and Jacob.

In embracing Zionism, Rav Soloveitchik was embracing all Jews, even those who don't embrace Torah.

Klinghoffer, however, shows no such love for his fellow Jews. His willingness to slough off the first covenant, of fate, to Christian Zionists again bespeaks a certain callousness of what purports to be a Jewish soul.

Finally, we get to the theological points.

Regarding homosexuality, Klinghoffer believes the state should share Paul's priorities. It should worry about homosexual sex, but not worry about forbidden foods, Sabbath violation or the ban on heterosexual sex during menstruation.

Regarding contraception, he presents a call for abstinence that again owes more to the New Testament than to Jewish jurisprudence. As far as the rabbis are concerned, Jewish men are the ones commanded with regard to procreation, leaving Jewish women to practice whatever contraception they choose.

So, too, on divorce, where he hews closer to Protestantism than to Judaism, and on the subordination of women to men, which is described as an ideal in the New Testament but in neither the Tanakh nor the Talmud.

Perhaps most distressing of all is the connection between this harsh Christian theology and the funders of Klinghoffer's employer, the Discovery Instititute, that we examined in the chapter on evolution. It is not just any Christian group that Klinghoffer affiliates with, but in particular a group with "Dominionist" inclinations, that is to say, a group that seeks to bring "Biblical law" to rule over America.

It is a project that if, God forbid, proved successful, would subvert America and America's role as a safe haven for half of the world's Jews.

And it is a project that Klinghoffer seems to be advancing as he sets out his own vision of Biblical America.

In favor of Klinghoffer's "Jewish" status, what do we have? A view on abortion that derives, in part, from the Talmud. Some rabbinic Torah commentaries. Really, rather slim pickings for an erstwhile Jewish thinker.

He's certainly not a proud Jew, one willing to stand by his people.

He seems more like a domesticated house Hebrew, willing to serve at the pleasure of his Christian masters.

So is Klinghoffer Jewish?

Who am I to judge?

15

God's Platform: How Would God REALLY Vote

Until now, we have examined the arguments brought by David Klinghoffer, and by turns analyzed, dissected, rebutted, refuted and ridiculed them.

Now it's time for God to seize the agenda.

What would be the key issues according to the Bible? Are there any burning issues that Klinghoffer missed?

Remember, the Bible and Jewish tradition indicate that the central role of government is the preservation of life and liberty. And yet, for Judaism the Torah is all about commandments. Six hundred and thirteen of them, according to the Talmud.

That's a lot to keep track of in a voting guide, let alone in a voting booth.

Luckily for the harried voter, the very same passage from the

Talmud (Makkot 24a) which numbers the commandments (248 do's, 365 don't's, for those keeping track) reduces them to more manageable numbers as well:

> David came and reduced them to eleven [principles], as it is written, "A Psalm of David. Lord, who shall sojourn in Thy tabernacle? Who shall dwell in Thy holy mountain? —
> [1] He that walks uprightly, and
> [2] works righteousness, and
> [3] speaks truth in his heart;
> [4] that has no slander upon his tongue,
> [5] nor does evil to his fellow,
> [6] nor takes up a reproach against his neighbor,
> [7] in whose eyes a vile person is despised, but
> [8] he honors them that fear the Lord,
> [9] he swears to his own hurt and changes not,
> [10] he puts not out his money on interest,
> [11] nor takes a bribe against the innocent. (Psalm 15) "

Doesn't bode well for the politics of negative campaigning, does it?

If eleven commandments prove too cumbersome, the Talmudic passage continues:

> Isaiah came and reduced them to six, as it is written,
> "[1] He that walks righteously, and
> [2] speaks uprightly,
> [3] He that despises the gain of oppressions,
> [4] that shakes his hand from holding of bribes,
> [5] that stops his ear from hearing of blood,
> [6] and shuts his eyes from looking upon evil; he shall dwell on high. (Isaiah 33:15-16)"

The Talmud continues:

> Micah came and reduced them to three as it is writ-
> ten, "It has been told you, O man, what is good, and
> what the Lord require of you:
> [1] only to do justly, and
> [2] to love mercy and
> [3] to walk humbly before thy God. (Micah 6:8)"

And further still:

> Again came Isaiah and reduced them to two, as it is
> said, "Thus says the Lord,
> [1] Keep justice and
> [2] do righteousness (Isaiah 56:1)"

Justice and righteousness. These are certainly good values to look
for in a candidate, a platform and a party. Good values, too, to demand
from our government, no matter who is elected.

What is missing in these lists of values are an array of "wedge" issues. Unlike the imperatives, values and directives that Republican
party strategists have placed front and center in recent years (and that
Klinghoffer placed at the forefront of his book)—gay marriage, most
notably, but also abortion, birth control, and evolution—the Talmud's
issues don't divide the electorate.

And of course, injustice and unrighteousness are what campaign
contributors pay the big bucks for. ("He that despises the gain of op-
pressions, that shakes his hand from holding of bribes," isn't a likely
recipient of donations from corporate lobbyists, no matter how much
Isaiah might stump for him.)

Klinghoffer began his book with the challenge: "Every election poses
a radical question. Will we vote with Him, or against Him?"

I'm going to vote *with* God. With the God that says: "Keep justice
and do righteousness."

And how will Klinghoffer vote? It is clear that he feels he also votes with God. But let us take a look at this dark God who gets Klinghoffer's ballot. This God delights in the spread of fear and division. This is the God who promotes enriching politicians through the taking of bribes, and a God who turns a deaf ear to poor people and to endangered species. This is a God who encourages those who make millions selling substandard ammunition to our troops overseas—and whose central goal since January 2001 has been to hide the truth, to cover up their actions and to deflect the attention of the American voter away from the terrible consequences caused by such deportment.

"Justice" and "righteousness" would require that you don't keep people in overseas prisons for years to avoid the embarrassment of having it made public that you have arrested them by mistake in the first place. The words of Isaiah and Micah are not based on any ideology about abortion or picking the Book of Samuel apart with a fine tooth comb to prove that a 20% tax rate is more kosher than a 32% tax rate.

The fact is, what God wants from His followers is what the American Constitution expects from its leaders:

> "…establish Justice, insure domestic Tranquility, provide for the common defence, promote the general Welfare, and secure the Blessing of Liberty to ourselves and our Posterity…"
> —Preamble to the United States Constitution

Our Talmudic passage finds its echo in these words of the founding fathers.

There is no big mystery here as to how God's will would play out in the realm of politics. The calls for justice and righteousness from Psalms, Isaiah and Micah, and James Madison answer the question of this book: How would God *really* vote?

About the Authors

YORI YANOVER is the author *The Cabalist's Daughter: A Novel of Practical Messianic Redemption* (2008), and of *Dancing and Crying* (1994), a behind-the-scenes look at the Lubavitch Hasidic movement, published in Hebrew. He has worked as an entertainer for the Israeli army, a taxi driver, and the first Jewish blogger. He now publishes *The Grand Street News*, a monthly print magazine serving his neighborhood, New York's Lower East Side.

LARRY YUDELSON is founder and editorial director of Ben Yehuda Press. He lives in Teaneck, N.J.

Also by Yori Yanover

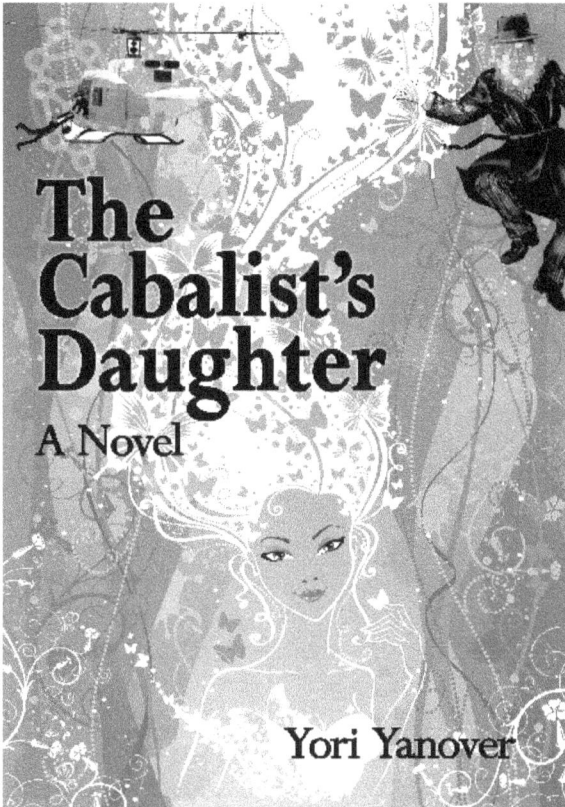

When the Master Cabalist of Brooklyn dies without an heir, it seems as if an age-old plot to bring the Messiah has failed.

But appearances can be deceiving.

Twenty years later, Nechama Gutkind leaves her cloistered home, determined to save the world—even if it kills her. For assistance, she turns to the Master's closest friend, 130-year-old Rabbi Lionel Abulafia. The last scion of a mystical dynasty, Abulafia has collected ancestral legend, mystical inspiration and wild speculation to create *The Cabalist's Handbook of Practical Messianic Redemption.*

Nechama's exploits attract followers and enemies from high and low. Firefights, helicopter battles and strange visions are only the beginning—because if the old rabbi is right, all Heaven is about to break loose!

AN EXCLUSIVE EXCERPT FROM

The Cabalist's Daughter
A NOVEL OF PRACTICAL MESSIANIC REDEMPTION

According to THE CABALIST'S HANDBOOK OF PRACTICAL MESSIANIC REDEMPTION, *the Spiritual Continuum of Everything* was formed on the second day of Creation:

> *It was a sad day, without question the saddest day in the history of the cosmos. On that day, the Creator, heretofore a single, unified and uninterrupted entity, gave birth to the possibility of two-ness.*
>
> *Duality was a terrible experience for the Creator. It brought about suspicion, uncertainty, misunderstanding, and self-centeredness. It tore right through the heart of God's simplicity. God could hardly bear it. For the billions upon billions of years which constituted the second day of Creation, God was searching for a good word He could say about the number Two, but none occurred to Him.*
>
> *God concluded that there was nothing good about Duality, other than the fact that it was all just a variant of Singularity. But even He didn't trust this concept completely.*
>
> *Only a mere eon or so later, God discovered the emanation of the possibility of measuring stuff. Of course this concept couldn't exist as long as one was the only known number, but the idea took on a life of its own as soon as two came into being.*
>
> *Like all things in the cosmos, as soon as it was possible to measure, measuring became the rage, and the Spiritual Continuum of Everything was already roaring with life. Except, of course, on the second day it had only one thing to measure: God/No God. Which explains why, as the second day was entering its billionth eon and God stumbled into the Spiritual Continuum of Everything, He was not very impressed, to say the least.*
>
> *God's mood changed only at the end of the Second Day, when He set out to create the Third Day. He was delighted with the concept of three-ness, because it held the promise of mitigation, of selection, and of conciliation. It also gave birth to the notion of Many, which God found particularly cheerful.*
>
> *Once He had created the concept of Three-and-Up, God had much more fun with the Spiritual Continuum of Everything. God saw the continuum*

as an expression of His constant desire to put things in perspective, a desire which forced an unintended result of Creation: the fact that everything in the cosmos was either to the right or to the left of everything else on the Continuum.

The further to the left things stood, the more they reflected God's penchant for making lists and setting up boundaries and judging.

The further to the right things were, the more open and available and merciful God's perceived qualities became.

So, for instance, Italian dictator Benito Mussolini (1883–1945) was more than a mile to the right of German mass-butcher Adolph Hitler (1889-1945), but only two and a half yards to the left of American film producer Cecil B. De Mille (1881-1959), known for his spectacular epics, The Ten Commandments and The Greatest Show on Earth.

Biblical tough guy, King Nebuchadnezzar (630-562 BCE), was surprisingly stationed a mere foot to the left of Hollywood bombshell Jayne Mansfield (1933-1967 CE).

And the thirty-ninth president of the United States, James Earl Carter Jr., was situated precisely one millimeter to the left of his own dinner jacket.

It can be safely stated that the Spiritual Continuum of Everything represented the first time God's dark side pulled a fast one on Him. It seduced the Creator with three-ness and all the delightful potential it bore for relationships between people and beaches and trees and race cars and watercress sandwiches—to the point where God had forgotten that Three was merely a very voluptuous Two.

The Creator understood that the Continuum represented His exile from Himself. He also acknowledged the Continuum as a creation of His Dark Aspect. This probably coincided with the moment that His Dark Aspect murmured sweetly, "Please fasten your seat belts, dinner will be served shortly. Thank you for flying Air Satan…"

Despite some popular notions that may suggest otherwise, Samael's place on the Spiritual Continuum of Everything is not directly opposite that of God's. His spot is precisely at the mid-point of that ever-expanding ethereal line. He is situated between the two most frightened men who ever lived: To Samael's left stands Eduard Bene (1884-1948), who lost his country Czechoslovakia to the Nazis in 1938, and to Samael's right stands Jan Masaryk (1886-1948), who lost his country Czechoslovakia to the Communists in 1948.

Ben Yehuda Press
Independent Orthodox books

Contemporary perspectives on the Book of Samuel

THE YESHIVAT CHOVEVEI TORAH RABBINICAL SCHOOL TANAKH COMPANION TO THE BOOK OF SAMUEL

Thirteen eye-opening close readings of the Book of Samuel offer refreshing new perspectives on familiar stories while always remaining true to the text. These essays combine modern techniques of literary scholarship with insights from midrash and subsequent classical Jewish Biblical scholarship. This highly readable volume provides a "big picture" understanding of the Book of Samuel through close attention to even the smallest details.

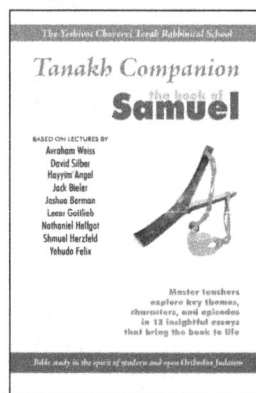

Discover life in Orthodoxy's suburban frontier

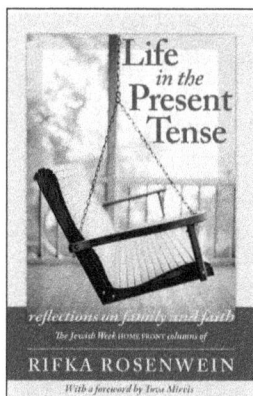

LIFE IN THE PRESENT TENSE: REFLECTIONS ON FAMILY AND FAITH
by **Rifka Rosenwein**

"A treasure trove of wisdom from one of American Judaism's most beloved and lamented vocies," — *Publishers Weekly*

"Dispatches from a life unfolding. Unwaveringly honest, wry, gentle, and reflective."—Tova Mirvis, author, *The Ladies Auxillary*

Rifka Rosenwein's column, "The Home Front," about her suburban, soccer-mom life, appeared at the back of *The New York Jewish Week* for seven years. Her reflections—on topics ranging from her son's first kindergarten girlfriend to lving on "cancer time"—are a death-defying celebration of life.

"Now I'll admit: Most parents watching their kids' Little League game don't start thinking about the Holocaust. That might just be me."

Ben Yehuda Press
Rediscovering classic Jewish thought

THE ESSENTIAL WRITINGS OF RABBI ABRAHAM ISAAC KOOK

Edited and translated by **Ben Zion Bokser**
"This work excels both in its judicious selection of texts and the quality of the translation. The reader is treated to Rav Kook's views on such topics as culture, evolution, scientific change, Torah study, holiness, morality and the Zionist revival. This volume enables readers to feel the pulse and power of this remarkable thinker."
—David Shatz, professor of philosophy, Yeshiva University

The Essential Writings of
Abraham Isaac Kook

Edited, Translated and Introduced by
Ben Zion Bokser

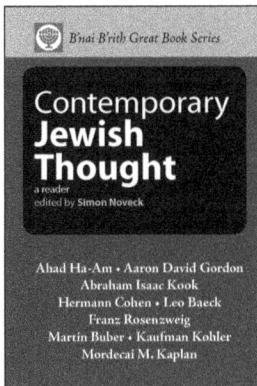

B'nai B'rith Great Book Series

Contemporary
Jewish
Thought
a reader
edited by Simon Noveck

Ahad Ha-Am • Aaron David Gordon
Abraham Isaac Kook
Hermann Cohen • Leo Baeck
Franz Rosenzweig
Martin Buber • Kaufman Kohler
Mordecai M. Kaplan

CONTEMPORARY JEWISH THOUGHT
THE B'NAI B'RITH GREAT BOOK SERIES
edited by **Simon Noveck**

Ben Yehuda Press is proud to bring this classic anthology of nine Jewish thinkers back into print. Featuring translated selections from the writings of Ahad Ha-am, Aaron David Gordon, Abraham Isaac Kook, Hermann Cohen, Leo Baeck, Franz Rosenzweig, Martin Buber, Kaufmann Kohler and Mordecai Kaplan. Published in cooperation with B'nai B'rith International.

AHRON'S HEART:
THE PRAYERS, TEACHINGS AND LETTERS OF AHRELE ROTH, A HASIDIC REFORMER
by **Rabbi Hillel Goelman and Rabbi Zalman Schachter-Shalomi**

For the first time, the writings and life of one of the 20th century's most important Hasidic thinkers are made available to a non-Hasidic English audience. To be published in Winter 2008.

Ben Yehuda Press
Experience the weekly Torah portion

Discuss Torah at your table
TORAH & COMPANY
by Judith Z. Abrams

Torah & Company
The weekly portion of Torah, accompanied by generous helpings of Mishnah and Gemara, served up with discussion questions to spice up your Sabbath table.

Judith Z. Abrams

"Reveals the power and relevance of each weekly Torah portion. A Shabbat treasure for every home." —Rabbi Goldie Milgram, author, *Reclaiming Judaism as a Spiritual Practice*

This useful book offers brief excerpts from each Torah portion, along with appropriately related selections from the Mishnah and Gemara—the "oral" Torah. Discussion questions for each selection are provided to spark open-ended conversation around dinner tables, and wherever else Jews gather to learn and argue.

The texts are short and provocative—the questions even more so. This book promises lively debate, where the deepest text of all is your learning partner.

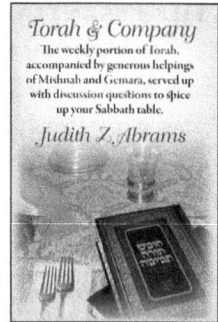

Discover a unique Jewish poet
FROM THE COFFEE HOUSE OF JEWISH DREAMERS:
POEMS OF WONDER AND WANDERING /
POEMS ON THE WEEKLY TORAH PORTION
by Isidore Century

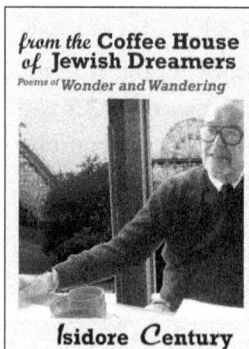

from the **Coffee House** *of* **Jewish Dreamers**
Poems of *Wonder and Wandering*

Isidore Century

"Isidore Century is a wonderful poet," says the *Jewish Week*, "funny, deeply observed, without pretension."

Says a reviewer at Librarything.com: "When I read the 'Poems of Wonder and Wandering,' I was awash in a sea of sadness and longing. Flip the book over and read 'Poems on the Weekly Torah Portion', and it is laugh out loud funny, full of tongue in cheek wit. It is the balance between sadness and humor, anger and joy, longing and acceptance, which makes this collection such a treasure."

Another reviewer agrees: "I am not a sophisticated reader of poetry. However, I absolutely love Isidore Century's collection. A treasure."

Ben Yehuda Press
Women who challenge the status quo

BESSIE SAINER. Bessie's "career" is full of hazards. At the age of twelve, she is exiled to Siberia because of her brothers' anti-czarist activities. At twenty-five, she loses her husband and baby girl to the ravages of civil war in revolutionary Russia.

At forty, she faces down Nazi hoodlums as she tries to disrupt a pro-Hitler rally in Madison Square Garden. At fifty-five, she is driven underground by McCarthyite persecution. At sixty-two, she squares off against racists in the South—and nearly loses the loyalty of her beloved daughter.

At eighty-eight, she is still making trouble and still making jokes.

A profoundly optimistic novel about a remarkable heroine—a rebel, a lover, a mother, a grandmother, a Jew, and an extraordinary human being.

Bessie: A Novel of Love and Revolution by **Lawrence Bush.**

KARIMA AL-TUSTARI. Charming and headstrong, Karimah is a young Karaite Jewish woman in 11th Century Egypt who follows her heart to live a life of adventure. Although unpredictable, Karimah is guided by her own steadfast ideas of honor and tradition.

Devastated, Karimah's father seeks comfort from Rabbi Nissim of North Africa, who responds with tales from classical rabbinic literature. Karimah, writing home to her brother, quotes not only from traditional Jewish texts, but also from the Arabian Nights.

As events unfold, the storytellers become lost in their own stories which begin to entwine and take on a life of their own. The storytellers learn that their tales are mirrors; the more they are told, the more they reflect the teller.

A Delightful Compendium: A Fabulous Tale of Romance, Adventure & Faith in the Medieval Mediterranean by **Burton**

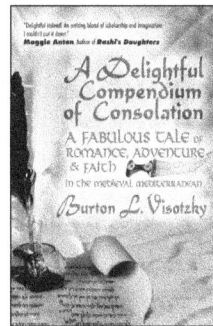

BenYehuda Press
Discover new Jewish spirituality

TORAH JOURNEYS: THE INNER PATH TO THE PROMISED LAND
by **Rabbi Shefa Gold**

Week by week, **Torah Journeys** makes the Torah personal, and the personal holy. Following the weekly Torah portion, readers are challenged to think about the Torah in terms of their own lives, and are guided to implement their own spiritual and personal growth.

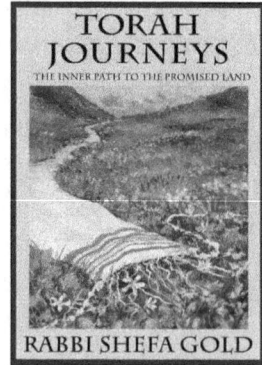

Hailed as one of the best Jewish books of 2006 by Beliefnet, and designated "the first Jewish Renewal Torah commentary" by the *New Jersey Jewish News,* **Torah Journeys** draws from diverse sources to create a new path of Divine challenge and blessing.

IN THE FEVER OF LOVE
AN ILLUMINATION OF THE SONG OF SONGS
by **Rabbi Shefa Gold**

"Shefa Gold, songstress and prophetess, here dares to reveal her heart, soul, and body in an intimate, erotic elaboration on the Song of Songs. But more than that: she audaciously proposes a Judaism whose ten commandments are mandates to love. In the Fever of Love is personal, daring, and drunk with God." —Jay Michaelson, author of *God in Your Body: Kabbalah, Mindfulness and Embodied Spiritual Practice*

"An amazing, loving and poetic commentary on this sacred text of the Song of Songs. A wonderful and awakening experience."

—David Cooper, author of *God is a Verb*

It is said that the whole of Torah could be derived from the Song of Songs. IN THE FEVER OF LOVE provides a poetic response to the Song of Songs, moving from the Biblical verses to a deeply personal, highly erotic meditation of love of God. A Jewish work of ecstatic religious literature in the tradition of the mystical poetess Mirabai.

Ben Yehuda Press
Remembering the American Jewish experience

THE WICKED WIT OF THE WEST:
GOLDEN AGE SCREENWRITER RECALLS HILARITY AND
HEARTACHES OF WORKING WITH GROUCHO, GARLAND,
GLEASON, BERLE, BURNS, BENNY AND MANY MORE
by **Irving Brecher** as told to **Hank Rosenfeld**

"The only good thing about making *At The Circus* was beginning my friendship with Irving Brecher." —Groucho Marx

Who is this Irving Brecher?

What was it like to be the only man ever to write two Marx Brothers movies by himself?

To be the last of the great MGM roundtable of screenwriters?

To be the famous unknown who wrote vaudeville and radio shows for Milton Berle, punched up *The Wizard of Oz*, and created "The Life of Riley"—on radio, in the movies, and as the very first television sitcom!

Once Hank met Irv, questions like these dogged him. And Hank dogged Irv. He couldn't get enough of Irv's rapid-fire patter and acid wit. This book is the product of 7 years of Hank's tagging along with Irv, splitting pastrami sandwiches, and hanging on Irv's every word.

Irv convinced Judy Garland to star in *Meet Me in St. Louis*, wrote *Bye Bye Birdie*, and gave Jackie Gleason his first TV series and a new set of teeth. The "Wicked Wit of the West" (as Groucho dubbed him) tells juicy tales about Hollywood legends John Wayne, L.B. Mayer, Jack Benny, George Burns, Ann-Margret, Ernie Kovacs, Cleo the bassett hound, and of course, Groucho, Harpo and Chico.

At 94, Irving Brecher finally gets the last word!

Coming in January, 2009, from Ben Yehuda Press.